Playground
Duty

Ned Manning is a teacher, writer, actor and script consultant. A past winner of the NSW Premier's Teachers' Scholarship, Ned has taught at Newtown High School of the Performing Arts, the EORA Centre for Aboriginal Visual and Performing Arts, Watson High School and Tenterfield High School. He was nominated for an AWGIE award for plays for young people in 2011, and his works have been performed around Australia and internationally. He has written plays for Bell Shakespeare's *Actors at Work* program and appeared in many film, TV and stage productions.

To all the students and teachers
who make teaching such a blast

73 Ormond Rd
Elwood
Victoria 3184

Dear Andrew,

How time flies! I've been meaning to drop you a line for ages but things keep getting away from me.

Life with two young children and a working Mum can get pretty hectic.

The Manning clan are descending on Yogyakarta to spend Christmas with Pud who is now in Sholomesia.

I have a website - nedmanning.com - so you can see what I'm up to!

I thought you might like a copy of my book. It seems to be going well. It is available online too so maybe I'll get a few overseas sales!

Elwood is next to St Kilda. A beautiful area, very like a country town.

Hope you are well.
                    Best Ned.

Playground
Duty

Dear Andrew,
Hope you enjoy it!.
love
Ned.

NED
MANNING

NEWSOUTH

'What a different and wonderful place the world would be if there were not only more teachers like Ned Manning, but more men like him. Open, humble, emotional, passionate, engaged, thoughtful and, above all, not afraid to look like an idiot!

This is an inspiring, funny and moving account of Ned's experiences as a teacher that looks honestly at the system, the students, the setbacks and successes, and the challenge of nurturing our precious kids.'

Noni Hazlehurst

A NewSouth book

Published by
NewSouth Publishing
University of New South Wales Press Ltd
University of New South Wales
Sydney NSW 2052
AUSTRALIA
newsouthpublishing.com

© Ned Manning 2012
First published 2012

10 9 8 7 6 5 4 3 2 1

National Library of Australia
Cataloguing-in-Publication entry
    Title: Playground duty/Ned Manning.
    ISBN: 978 174223 316 1 (pbk.)
    Subjects: Manning, Ned – Anecdotes.
        Teaching – Anecdotes.
        Teachers – Anecdotes.
        Education – Anecdotes.
    Dewey Number: 371.1

Design Josephine Pajor-Markus
Cover design Sandy Cull, gogoGingko
Cover images Author photograph by Sandy Cull; additional images iStockphoto
Printer Griffin Press

This book is printed on paper using fibre supplied from plantation or sustainably managed forests.

Contents

Author's note

All the events and characters in this book are real. Everything I talk about really happened. All the characters are people I came across in my travels as a teacher.

Because of the nature of some of the issues discussed, however, I have deliberately moved some incidents and moments to protect the people involved. While the book is chronological in the way it charts my journey as a teacher, not all the events occurred in the exact order that they appear in the book. In many ways what happened is more important than when or where it happened.

While this is a work of non-fiction I have used real names selectively. I have used real names only where the person in question is a public figure. Some characters are an amalgam of two people, which was another reason for using fictional names. Some people may recognise themselves or have fun guessing who other people might be.

Playground Duty is not really a memoir. It is not about me and my innermost thoughts but about what I saw and experienced. It is a book about the world of teaching, a world all of us have encountered. I have used my experiences to talk about what really happens in staffrooms, classrooms and, yes, the playground.

I am indebted to every student, every teacher and every ancillary staff member who I have had the pleasure to come across in what seems like a lifetime of teaching. Writing the book made me realise that I wouldn't have missed it for quids.

Prologue:
Duty of care

I'm standing at Sydney Airport, preparing for a flight to China. The nervous tension that precedes any overseas trip is coursing through my veins. Have I got the tickets? Have I got my passport? Have I filled in my departure card? There is something else though, which adds a certain *frisson* to the whole experience: I'm not travelling alone. I'm travelling with 200 teenagers from the Sydney region. We're embarking on a cultural exchange starting in Shanghai and then moving on to Yangzhou, Nanjing, Zhengzhou and Dengfeng. We'll be performing pieces of music, drama and dance. We'll be playing in arts centres, theatres and schools. It's a tour and it's a biggie. It's referred to as the 'Expanding Horizons' project. 'Exploding Horizons' might be more accurate.

One hundred of these teenagers are from the school where I teach drama, Newtown High School of the Performing Arts. Eighty of them are music students and make up choirs, orchestras, string quartets, percussion groups and assorted bands. The other 20 are drama students. *My* drama students. We're going to perform a piece we've devised which can be best described as an impressionistic history of Australia in 15 minutes. And we're going to be performing it to people who have, at most, barely heard of Australia and almost certainly know nothing about Australian history.

So here I am with a bunch of teenagers ranging in age from 14 to 17 for whom I'm going to be responsible over the next fortnight. Personally responsible. Touring China. Twenty teenagers. Twenty-four/seven, as they say. I notice my heart is beating a little faster than usual and I'm feeling a bit queasy in the stomach.

What was I thinking? On my last trip to Shanghai I discovered I was barely able to look after myself. On that occasion I accepted a generous offer from two 'students' for a guided tour of the city. Little did I realise that they were after a bit more than an opportunity to practise their English. I escaped intact and fortunately no one here knows about that.

My charges are an interesting mix. The bulk of them are in Year 11. They are 16 or 17, full of energy and on the lookout for a good time. A good time that might not be limited to walking around museums. To say many of them are party animals would not be an exaggeration. The others – the Year 10s and 9s – are variously excited, nervous or already homesick. One of them won't stop talking from the moment we leave to the moment we return. These guys are under my 'duty of care'.

'Duty of care' is one of those wonderful departmental phrases that are trotted out to remind teachers of their responsibilities. When you forget to do PGD (playground duty) you are abrogating your 'duty of care'. And if some kid falls over and scratches his knee you can be sued because you have failed in your 'duty of care'.

Being a bit old-school, I've never been into the jargon that has insinuated itself into every aspect of teaching, or 'pedagogy' as we now like to call it. We've gone from using simple language to describe what we are doing to using phrases that are, at best, bizarre. For instance, 'value adding'. I sat in a staff meeting where I was told we were 'value adding' the kids. *Value adding?* I thought we were teaching them.

Anyway, I'm standing at the check-in counter with 20 high-octane teenagers ready to rock and roll in China. The ratio was meant to be 1 to 15, that is, one teacher for every 15 kids. Someone in the department had worked that out. It probably took them a year and several hundred meetings/conferences to come up with 1 to 15 as the most appropriate ratio for 'duty of care'. Fortunately my boss – our school principal – or someone else in charge has agreed that, as I have 20 in my performance group, I may as well be responsible for them all. To be honest, the full implications of this trip haven't quite dawned on me yet. But they soon will.

I start counting heads. Roll call has never been my strong point. Truants can have a field day in my classes if they want to. It's not that I don't understand the need for roll call, it's just that I tend to get into it – the *teaching* – before I remember to call the roll. And any teacher worth their salt will soon work out who's likely to truant and who isn't. But this is different. I need to know that all my charges are 'present and accounted for'. Fortunately, I can count to 20 so I gather them around me and count heads. There should be 20, but there are only 19. Bugger. Great start! I try again. Still 19. Who's missing?

'Call the roll, sir.'

'Thanks for that, Kevin.'

Kevin's the one who never stops asking questions, giving advice or stating the bleeding obvious. I love him, but …

I call the roll. Kate's not here. Kate? One of the smartest and most reliable kids I've ever taught.

'Where's Kate?'

Everyone starts panicking. Teenagers love panicking – it's part of the teen DNA. I try to exude calm but, to be honest, I'm getting a bit toey. Time is ticking away. I've lost one of the kids I'm responsible for and we haven't even gone through the departure gate.

It's starting to dawn on me that this isn't going to be like the overseas travelling I've grown to love so much. Just as I'm beginning to wonder what I've got myself in for I see Kate pushing her way through the crowd, parents in tow. She's looking pretty shame-faced.

'Slept in.'

Kate's an interesting mix of teenager and adult. Mature beyond her years but a teenager all the same, she's got a wicked sense of humour and, I'm soon to discover, is not exactly the shrinking violet she pretends to be.

We're called to the departure gate. Time for goodbyes. Then it hits me like a ton of bricks: I'm responsible for 20 apples of adoring parents' eyes. Some of the parents are teary. A few fix me with looks that leave nothing to the imagination.

You'd better look after my precious jewel.

Others look at me quizzically as they shake my hand.

Are you up to this?

Paranoia kicks in. Am I? Then the thought, 'Maybe they don't trust me.' Maybe I don't trust myself …

One last roll call before we go through the gate. A flash of genius! I think it's mine, but it might be from one of the kids, probably Kevin. We'll number off like they do in those American war movies. I allocate numbers. One to 20. We try it out – disaster. Half of them forget their numbers. I smile pathetically as the parents look on. We try again. It almost works, like a barely oiled machine. I'm really filling these parents with confidence. They wave anxious goodbyes as we make our way to the gate.

Once we're through the gate there is Customs to negotiate. Customs is always a pain but when you've got 20 in your family it's something else again. I watch different kids fumbling for passports, dropping boarding passes, finding themselves in the wrong queue and the penny starts to drop: this is going to be one hell of a trip!

We make it to the departure lounge and I grab a coffee. The kids are like lambs let loose in a paddock for the first time. They're already kicking up their heels. Their collective demeanour has transformed. Gone is the bored 'over it' disposition they put on for mum and dad. Now there is no masking their sheer excitement. This is what they have been waiting for. To get away, to be free, to be *themselves*.

It's always bemused me how different kids are when you see them with their parents. Parent–teacher nights are a classic example. The vibrant, enthusiastic student I've come to know and love suddenly becomes withdrawn and long-suffering when in the presence of an inquiring parent. They squirm. They roll their eyes. They look like they're having their teeth pulled. It makes you realise what a privilege it is to see them as they really are. Or at least one aspect of what they really are. One thing is for sure, we teachers see the best of kids. Admittedly, sometimes the worst as well, but the best outstrips the worst, by a huge margin. It's why teaching is such a great job.

Parents are interesting in this context too. Some of them regress to become the students they once were. Or wish they were. Or pray their kids will become. They're all perfect manners and respectful nods. Like most things about teaching, it's slightly schizophrenic. Good friends have taken to calling me 'Mr Manning' when we meet at parent–teacher night. These are people I've partied with till all hours. Schools have a very strange effect on everyone, not just on those who work in them. Then there are parents who inquire:

'How on earth do you put up with her?'

Sitting in front of me is a kid I'd trust with my life and her mum or dad asks me a question like that. *Put up with her?* What are they talking about? She's a champion human being. This is what I mean about us seeing the best of kids. I never get attitude from this girl. Never.

Of course there are other parents, the ones who turn up a little bit stoned, half-pissed or even totally off their face. They sit down, eyes barely open or, depending on their poison, darting in a thousand directions. It's quite disconcerting. So is the breath of the parent who has downed six schooners on the way.

But these parents are doing their best; it mightn't be very good, but at least they're there. And you come to understand why their kid might be struggling or, on the other hand, to marvel at how on earth they've been doing so well. Of course if the kid happens to be there too, which is rare, they give you a 'Can you believe it?' look or spend the whole interview staring at the floor.

The worst type of parent, though, is the one who believes their child is a genius/prodigy/saint/potential national hero or some other figment of their overly fertile imagination. They are impossible. Of course they think I'm an idiot/bludger/narcissist/imposter if I don't agree. Maybe they're right.

Back in the departure lounge we're finally called to board. We seem to have been waiting for hours. Waiting – something we're going to get used to on this trip.

The flight is uneventful. In-flight movies, iPods, books, magazines, cards, endless chatter and occasional sleep variously occupy the kids. It's a long flight and there has been a delay, which means we're running a bit late for our connecting flight from Guangzhou to Shanghai. Our tour guide for this leg is a fairly excitable Chinese national called Wally, who talks incredibly quickly and waves his hands around when things look like veering off course. Wally's starting to panic about the connecting flight. I'm not too fussed – what can you do about situations you have no control over?

'Go with the flow,' I say to the kids. They grin. It's all part of the ride to them.

To tell the truth, 'panic' may be understating Wally's response to things that don't go exactly to plan. I'm not sure if a word has been invented to adequately capture his, let's say, excitability. In any case it appears someone told him that the louder you yell the quicker a problem will be solved. So by the time we arrive in Guangzhou, once know as Canton, Wally is beside himself. He tears around the airport waving his arms furiously, shouting at the top of his lungs and pointing a lot. This tactic is both amusing and surprisingly effective. We're ushered through gates and literally run to the luggage carts specially commandeered to transport us to the connecting flight. For the local Chinese it must be quite a sight. A hundred Western kids and their teachers sprinting after their hyped-up tour guide. The kids are loving it. Not only are we saved a considerable hike to the gate but we get to career around the terminal on carts. It's like a joyride at a theme park.

Wally's obviously got influence because the flight is held just for us. This mightn't endear us to the other passengers but no one complains. I can't imagine a domestic flight in Australia being held for a group of visiting Chinese kids. We're being afforded special treatment.

I figure that a friendship with Wally might be worth cultivating. I sit next to him in the vain hope of getting some special privileges. Like *cold* beer. We chat away and he tells me the government are very supportive of this tour. The Chinese government? Maybe this isn't just any old school trip.

He also tells me it's the Festival of the Moon, a celebration dating back 3000 years. He explains its significance. It strikes me how genuinely proud he is of his culture. We are served moon cakes on the flight as a special treat. The kids aren't all that keen on them, although once we explain their significance, they do their best to pretend to enjoy them. Kate offers me her second one and watches while I diplomatically scoff it down. Wally is delighted. He asks if I'd like more. How can I refuse?

The excitement is mounting as we fasten our seat belts for the descent into Shanghai. The plane touches down and there is a collective cheer. And clapping. On some flights this might be seen as congratulating the flight crew but I suspect our kids are cheering because they're ready to rip. Even though it's been a long day, they aren't showing any signs of flagging. Quite the opposite, in fact.

We disembark and make our way to Customs. It's clear a good percentage of this trip will involve queuing and counting. We do a head count; that is, we number off. We're getting the hang of it now. And we – they – have added a little beat to the routine. Not just any beat, it's a funky little beat. And it involves a bit of a dance step as well. We are a performing arts high school after all. Roll call as performance art – that's my kind of roll call. We attract a bit of attention as we start the clapping; everyone within earshot looks around to see what's going on. The kids have named us 'Team Ned'. Any members of Team Ned who might have strayed hear the beat and rush back to join us. In theory anyway. The beat becomes our signature tune. Later on the music kids will try to emulate us – as if! We're *drama*! We're the best! Not that it's a competition.

Heads counted, we pass through Customs into another queue to collect our bags. Then another queue for the bus. This is what I'm here for: to corral kids into queues for this and that and everything. Thank God I've got experience in this sort of thing. I'm a farm boy, it reminds me of counting sheep through a gate. Shepherding my flock.

The bus trip to the hotel is fantastic. Even though I've been to Shanghai before, seeing it through the eyes of a teenager is another thing entirely. We're all pretty pumped. It's an amazing city, especially at night. Everyone is straining to see what's going on. Cameras and iPhones record every moment. The bus is buzzing. It strikes me that the kids are interested. Really interested. Because it's the Festival of the Moon the place is lit up like a Christmas tree. There are lanterns everywhere. It's quite a sight.

'Look at that!'

They rush to one side of the bus to take it all in.

'Hey guys, look at this, that old guy's carrying a fridge on the back of his bike!'

They rush to the other side.

We get to the hotel and unload. Not just bags but musical instruments as well. Instruments for 80 musicians. There seems to be every instrument imaginable. It turns out some of them have been damaged. Badly. This could be a disastrous beginning to the trip. Some of the kids are really upset; their instruments aren't cheap and they value them personally. They're worried their parents will be angry with them or they won't be able to play. The music teachers show enormous sensitivity in handling a potentially explosive situation.

'It's okay, we'll find replacements,' says Dylan, the Welsh violin wizard.

How? It's well after midnight and none of us speaks Chinese. Dylan is in earnest discussion with Gavin, Wally's replacement for this leg. Gavin's a bit calmer than Wally.

The hotel foyer is abuzz. Some kids are lining up to get their room keys, others are trying to exchange money. The hotel receptionists don't speak English. One of our kids is Chinese and suddenly becomes very popular. Us teachers are collecting and checking passports. We're counting heads. We're answering a thousand questions coming from all directions.

Some of the younger kids are starting to fade. The older ones look like they're ready to party. The hotel's tiny shop is jam packed with kids. Everyone is talking at once. Over in a corner Gavin is on the phone. He's nodding patiently. We start shepherding the kids to their rooms. The lift is struggling. It takes about ten at a time. With the amount of luggage some of them have brought, it takes about five. They've all bought enough luggage for a world tour. On a ship. A container ship. This is going to take hours. At this rate we'll never get to bed. Some of the kids decide to lug their bags up the stairs. The stairs aren't carpeted.

Ker-clunk, ker-clunk, ker-clunk.

About 50 take the stairs option. You'd want your money back if you booked in for a quiet night. I hope no one's in the honeymoon suite. This isn't a tour, it's an invasion.

Finally we get the kids to their rooms. Check-in has taken a couple of hours and we're exhausted. Dylan and I settle down for a well-earned night cap. Bernie, another musical maestro, joins us. Gavin comes over. Somehow at this time of night he has arranged replacement instruments for tomorrow's concert. The music staff have been politely insistent, but insistent all the same; they know how important this is to their kids. This is the first of many insights I get into the resourcefulness of the music department. They are, quite simply, powerhouses. They never stop. They seem to have no concern for their own comfort. Their entire focus is on getting what is best for their kids, or the best sound out of their kids. To have them performing at the highest level possible.

That's the thing about 90 per cent of teachers: they want their kids to do the best they possibly can. Some might seem like fascists, some might be mean-spirited, some might not be great at being warm and fuzzy, but the vast majority of them want what's best for their kids. I have yet to meet a teacher who wants their kids to fail. Teachers employ as many different methods as they have person-alities to get the desired result for their kids. This is something that is completely missed in the wider education debate.

How do you define a good teacher? You won't find the answer on a mark sheet, or in a league table, or on a roll of honour. Or in a newspaper headline. You'll find it when you see them doing everything in their power to get hold of a tuba at 1.30 in the morning in a foreign city where they don't speak the language.

And not giving up till they do.

It's now 3.30 and we're ready to call it a night. We've taken turns to check the corridors and all seems in order. Most lights are out. There's a bit of chat from some rooms but it's pretty innocent and to be expected.

Dylan volunteers to do one last run-around to check all is well. As we wearily collect our bags he returns looking concerned. He signals for me to follow him. There's been some smoking. What should we do? It's the first night – we could go in hard and threaten to send them home. We could scream and shout and report them to higher authorities. We could have them stripped of their privileges and tell them they're not performing tomorrow.

We could, but we don't. We decide to handle it ourselves, firmly but reasonably. After all, haven't we been there ourselves? The culprits own up. They've *owned their own behaviour*. We remind them of their responsibilities and point out that we're disappointed in them and that they've let us and themselves down. Then we send them to bed, in their own rooms.

Finally, finally we stumble off ourselves.

We wake the next morning to a traditional Chinese breakfast. Not a Weet-Bix in sight. The kids file down, most looking a bit shell-shocked but ready for the day. We are scheduled to go to the World Expo. In fact, I thought we were performing at the World Expo. I thought that was the point of the trip. That's what it said on the website. Something seems to have got lost in translation.

Oh well. *Go with the flow.*

Quite organically, the teachers have all taken on different roles; that is, apart from our designated roles as directors, conductors and carers. It's like clockwork. Everything is covered. It's great because someone tells me what to do and where to go. It's a grown-up game of follow-the-leader. No one throws their weight around. No one complains and everyone does whatever is needed.

World Expo is going to be big. We're carting a hundred kids around World Expo on a public holiday, the day when it breaks all daily attendance records. Nearly a million people will join us. So there are going to be lots of queues and lots waiting. There is also going to be lots of potential for something to go horribly wrong, like someone losing their passport, or being pick-pocketed, or getting lost, or just about anything. And it's raining. Of course, very few of us have raincoats or umbrellas.

The buses arrive and we climb on board. We're given designated buses. Team Ned has its own bus, which we generously share with a few music kids and Frances, another of the fabulous music staff. This will be our bus for the whole tour. It even has a number: Number 10 Bus! The kids are handed their lunch boxes. It really is a school trip. I haven't done this for ... well ... ever.

'Team Ned number off!'

'All present and accounted for, sir!'

Although no one says that. It's not that kind of trip.

We arrive at World Expo. It's not just big – it's huge. Getting there through Shanghai's traffic has been an experience in itself. I've never seen so many people in one place. The queues stretch for miles and miles. The odds of getting lost or, worse, losing someone have shortened dramatically.

We file out and head towards the Australian Pavilion. Apparently we're getting special treatment, again, and our queues will be smaller than those the general public have to endure.

Just being in a crowd this size is wild enough, but in a city like this, with the noise and the smells and the general energy of the place, it's simply mind-blowing. We huddle together under the few umbrellas we have and do our best to keep dry. The kids are unfailingly good-humoured about this. They are wired; they're up for anything. And that could be a problem. Lots to see, lots of ways to go missing. We number off again. And again. We'd better enjoy this routine because we're going to be doing enough of it!

We make it to the Australian Pavilion, which looks like a rusty silo. And that's the best bit. We follow the walkway, which kind of spirals upwards, and on the walls are snapshots of 'Aussie life'. We all live on a beach or a farm. We're unfailingly cheerful and fit – man, we're the fittest nation on earth. And our teeth! That fluoride has really kicked goals. Everyone is flashing Colgate smiles.

Indigenous culture is there in a typically tokenistic way. Henry, a Year 11 boy with a keen sense of social justice, sidles up to me.

'Can you believe this?' he asks, shaking his head. We are reading *The Seven Stages of Grieving* in class. It's like it has never been written.

'This is a bad Year 7 project,' says Joanna, one of the nicest and most perceptive Year 10 girls on the planet. And it is. It's jingoistic and devoid of any of the things that make us vaguely interesting as a culture. Here we are, a bunch of Australians in Shanghai looking at someone else's idea of us. Only it's not us. Not even close.

'Who's Banjo?' asks Taraka.

Exactly.

Kids have the most amazing bullshit barometers. They can pick it from miles off. And this is bullshit. They're polite about it because we're visitors but they're way too sophisticated to be impressed with this nonsense. As for the teachers, we just shake our heads. We teach kids to be analytical. We encourage them to be critical. We try to avoid patronising them or bullshitting them.

When we reach the top we are herded into an auditorium for an interactive display of 'Aussie life'. Looks pretty cool. Our hopes are raised.

'This is more like it.'

Then an enthusiastic MC comes out and revs the audience up.

'Aussie Aussie Aussie! Oi oi oi!'

'What?'

I look at Dylan. He's covering his head. He can't look. The Chinese in the crowd join the chant, probably out of politeness. We just squirm. Dylan's orchestra are going to perform the first movement of Schubert's unfinished Symphony No. 8 and the best the organisers of the Aussie Pavilion can come up with to represent us is this crap? It's excruciating. The content is straight from a 1950s tourist brochure offering sunny skies and lots of open spaces. The only things missing are Chips Rafferty and kangaroos.

It's bitterly disappointing and our kids can't get out of there quick enough. We rush past the 'Aussie' stalls – offering football, meat pies and Holden cars, vegemite and probably Namatjira tea towels – and emerge into the sunlight and the real world. We're all feeling stunned and a bit embarrassed. We number off.

'Where's 13?'

Hayley. I panic. My worst nightmare. I've lost someone on day one. I send them off in pairs to scout for her. After a while she saunters back licking an ice cream. We glare at her.

'What?'

Heart-attack material.

We've got a bit of time on our hands before we make our way to the Chinese Pavilion. I have a bright idea.

'Guys, how about we do our piece?'

They look at me like I'm mad.

'Where?'

'Here.'

They laugh.

'Seriously. There's enough space.'

Plenty of people are already looking at us. It won't be hard to draw a crowd.

'A bit of street theatre.'

'We haven't got our costumes. Or our bamboo sticks.'

'Or my clapping sticks,' says Kevin.

'That's okay. You can just clap.'

They know me. They think I'm mad, which means they know I'm not joking. I've told them our challenge is to perform our piece at least once a day while we're in China. Besides, weren't we meant to perform at the World Expo? This is our big chance. They look at each other. Some shake their heads.

'No way.'

Others, the more adventurous ones, are coming around. It's got nothing to do with age, this capacity to take risks. It mightn't even have much to do with parenting. Some kids, no matter what age, will have a go at anything, and I'm not talking about alcohol or drugs or what adults think risk-taking means with kids. They put themselves on the line. They have a go. They aren't afraid of what people think of them. They have it in their bones.

The kids look at each other, they look at me, they grin.

'Why not?' asks Chloe.

'Why not indeed!'

They gather into a huddle. The recalcitrants are dragged in by the weight of popular opinion. Some give me the 'You're a dick-head' look. I smile back.

Our piece begins with everyone linking arms and forming what might be a huge rock, perhaps Uluru. It's about the beginning of time. They start gently heaving. It's like the rock is coming to life. I look around. People are watching. Lots of people. They gather on walkways, on steps, wherever they can get a view. They crowd around us, at least ten deep. I'm engulfed. Wherever I look I see inquisitive faces. I can't get the grin off my face.

The rock opens up, like a giant lily. They twist out, eyes searching as they are released. After they've all been set loose a single boy emerges from the centre, the earth. He's Indigenous. He claps them awake. They pick up the beat. They start clapping. A rhythm starts up. Stamping feet accompany the rhythm.

The crowd is mesmerised. This is one of those unexpected, exhilarating moments that you might experience in teaching. It is raw, honest, real. No lights, no music, no costumes. Just a bunch of kids giving it their all.

As the piece continues it becomes obvious that they have this huge audience in the palm of their hands. Cameras are flashing, people are pushing me out of the way to get a better look. It is *so cool*. As they explode out of a waltz and into some hip-hop the crowd goes nuts. The reaction is out of this world. Then the final tableau:

'*Nee haoww!!*'

'Hello' in Mandarin. The crowd erupts.

The kids are instant rock stars. They are on fire. Grins as wide as Sydney Harbour, they are surrounded by 'fans' asking for photos, autographs, handshakes.

I can't believe it. My eyes are watering. I had not expected this, nor had anyone else. This is what can happen when you embrace the world of the unexpected. The world of teaching.

Time is a Traveller

False start

Someone handed me the telegram. It was the one I'd been dreading.

I'd been a Teacher's Scholarship holder, which meant that I had a bond with the New South Wales Department of Education. They had paid my university fees and provided me with a living allowance; in return I was theirs to send anywhere in the state once I'd graduated. New South Wales is a big state and if you didn't like where you were sent you could resign and pay off your bond. But that wasn't an option for me – I wanted to be a teacher.

Everyone at university prayed they'd be sent to the North Coast. If you got sent there, the chances were you'd never leave. That's why a lot of good schools or schools in good locations have very old teachers, and conversely why a lot of schools in outer suburbs and country towns have very young teachers.

I had initially been sent to Gunnedah in north-eastern New South Wales. If you were going to be sent anywhere, Gunnedah seemed like a pretty good place. It is 475 kilometres (or 295 miles – back in 1973 we measured distances in miles) from Sydney. This was only about 200 miles, or three hours, from where I'd gone to university in Newcastle, which meant I could return for a weekend if I needed some 'city lights'. I could even go home to our farm near Rylstone. So although Gunnedah was in the country it was not isolated. It was geographically perfect. It was also beautiful country:

Gunnedah was where Dorothea Mackellar wrote the iconic poem 'My Country', popularly known as 'I Love a Sunburnt Country'.

I began as a support teacher. This was a time when there were more graduating teachers than there were permanent positions, but part of the scholarship–bond deal meant that we had to be sent somewhere, so we were sent to schools that already had a full complement of teaching staff. Being a support teacher was good because you didn't have a full load and could ease yourself into the role of full-time teacher. It was like an on-the-job apprenticeship, one step up from being a student or 'prac' teacher, all care and little responsibility. The major drawback with being a support teacher was that you could be transferred at the drop of a hat, but I didn't consider this a possibility; for some reason I was confident a permanent position would soon come up in Gunnedah.

Before I knew it I was standing in front of a Year 9 English class talking about creative writing. The kids were receptive and I was convinced that, in my hands, they would become literary geniuses. My Year 11 class were only about three years younger than me and we clicked immediately. The playground was friendly and as I walked across it I sensed that I was being noticed. I enjoyed the attention. It was a new feeling and good for a young man's ego. My mentor on the English staff wisely counselled a little less self-assuredness, but of course I knew better. I was going to change the world and Gunnedah seemed like a good place to start.

I was eagerly awaiting Wednesday sport. Taking sport was, and still is, as much a part of a teacher's duties as playground duty. Some teachers railed against it but I soon learned that it was a great way to get to know the kids. I also learned that I loved coaching it nearly as much as playing it.

The tradition at Gunnedah before sport was to head down the local for a counter lunch. I followed my elders and betters to the bar and when I saw they were having a schooner I decided I'd better have one too. The coach of the senior footy team, a man I thought I should impress, offered me a second. And a third. He walked out of the pub as sober as a judge; I stumbled out like a drunken sailor. I think the old hands might have been literally taking the piss out of me.

I was happy with life in Gunnedah. There was a good mix of down-to-earth country types, the sort I'd grown up with, and young 'radicals' like myself who embraced the social revolution that was taking place in the early 1970s. I'd been there six weeks and had settled in well; I'd made friends, begun playing footy and, having done the obligatory few weeks living in the pub, found a flat and moved in. Everything was shaping up pretty well.

Then I opened the telegram. It read: *You have been transferred to Tenterfield*, or words to that effect. My heart sank. Transferred. Just as I was finding my feet.

I'd been offered a permanent position. Wasn't this what everyone wanted? Security? Tenure? Not me. I'd fallen in love with Gunnedah and I didn't want to go anywhere. I didn't even notice the bit about a permanent position; all I saw was '*transferred*'. Then I saw where: Tenterfield.

'Where's Tenterfield?'

That's how ignorant I was. All I knew of Tenterfield amounted to a little picture of Henry Parkes giving his legendary Federation address that appeared in the top left-hand corner of my history book at school. I looked it up on a map. It looked like the end of the earth, right up on the Queensland border and miles from anywhere. I was devastated. I pleaded with the relevant authorities but my words fell on deaf ears. The boss or headmaster of Gunnedah – now known as the principal – told me he'd love to have me back if a vacancy came up. I'm sure he said that to everyone …

So after much wailing and gnashing of teeth, I packed all my worldly goods into my VW Beetle and headed off towards Tenterfield. For the second time in six weeks I was re-locating, but this time I had no idea about where I was going or what I was in for.

On probation

Shortly before I began teaching I saw *Wake in Fright*. It's a classic Australian movie about a teacher who, like me, was on a bond and sent to the outback. He was naïve and idealistic but had his illusions shattered by the brutality of life on the fringes. It's a wonderful film but seemed far removed from the civilised world I enjoyed in Gunnedah. For some reason I was reminded of *Wake in Fright* as I drove up the New England Highway towards Tenterfield. I sensed I was heading well beyond my comfort zone.

Tenterfield was on top of the granite belt. It was mountainous, rugged country and great boulders lined the horizon. It was country where you could lose yourself, get lost, or hide. Bushranger country. Thunderbolt hung out there. It made me think of *Deliverance*.

To be honest, I was intimidated. Going to Gunnedah had been exciting. It might have been challenging to move away from friends and into a new phase of life, but it wasn't scary. This was different; I was charting very unfamiliar territory. I was barely 22, I'd lived a pretty sheltered existence and I wasn't sure I was up to it. I convinced myself I'd return to Gunnedah at the earliest opportunity.

I drove into Tenterfield and straight out the other side before I realised it. I swung a U-turn and headed back into town. It was a Sunday. It was like a ghost town; you could have fired a cannon down the main street and not hit a soul. I searched for signs of life but there didn't seem to be any. This was not a great start.

I had the address of the principal. He lived on High Street, just off the main drag and next to the school. I located his house and knocked on the door. An old guy opened it. I thought I had the wrong address.

'I'm looking for Mr Foster.'

'You've found him.' He looked me up and down with a resigned smile. 'You must be the new science teacher.'

'No. I'm English/history …'

'Here's your timetable. I'll see you tomorrow.'

And he closed the door.

I looked at the timetable. Science? Woodwork? *Metalwork?* I'd been thrown out of science at school for not taking it seriously. I'd made a tray in woodwork at primary school, but it took a year and the teacher did most of the work. As for metalwork …

I thought I was hallucinating. I looked around. Across the road was an oval but it looked abandoned. No one was running around or kicking a ball. There was no activity at all. Nothing, not even a stray dog to talk to. I looked up and down High Street. Deserted. I considered going back and knocking on the principal's door again but something told me it would be a waste of time. Even though he was a kindly man, it was pretty clear that Mr Foster didn't want to talk to me. Not today. Not on Sunday.

So this was it.

I needed somewhere to stay. I did a 'lap' of the main street, explored a few side-streets and eventually found a pub. The Royal. (What else?) The friendly publican gave me a knowing smile and a key.

'A lot of teachers stay here. When they first arrive.'

There was something about his delivery that seemed odd. I soon learned that people in Tenterfield didn't waste words.

Understated is an understatement.

I threw my bag inside. The room at The Royal didn't do much for my mood. It was a bit bleak; in fact, the whole situation was bleak. I'd left a really positive start to my teaching career behind and I now found myself in some godforsaken place on top of the granite belt facing the prospect of teaching subjects I knew nothing about. There was no one to talk to: the main bar was empty, the main street was empty. I was pretty forlorn.

I found a public phone box and called home. To add insult to injury, I'd planned a weekend with my new girlfriend at our farm. She was coming from Canberra but I'd just gone a couple of hundred miles in the other direction. My old man picked up the phone. I could hear voices and laughing. A long lunch was in progress. He didn't give me a lot of sympathy.

'Smarten up.'

He hung up. I stood there with the receiver in my hand, staring through the little window in the phone box, and I lost it. What was going on? I'd been so excited about going teaching. I'd gone to DJ's and bought myself some new shirts – body shirts were all the rage in those days. I'd bought new ties, shorts and, yes, long socks. I had complete matching sets: for example, mauve body shirt, maroon tie. So adult. So cool. So 1973.

I took my new calling very seriously. I'd even given up sugar and salt after a health lecture at university alerted us to the deleterious effects those two evils could have on young bodies. I'd never been a serious smoker but they were out the window too – no more early-morning gasper with a cup of coffee. I was going to get really fit. I was going to limit my drinking to 'a few' on special occasions and, after that embarrassing episode at Gunnedah, never during school hours. I was to be the exemplar of first-year-out teachers, a role-model for the youth of the nation.

So why was I being banished to the Queensland border? The

debut season of my inevitably stellar career had been cruelly cut short. I'd been transferred to the Wild West or, more accurately, the Wild North-West and every door was slammed shut. Not for the last time I retired to bed, covered my head with my pillow and had a good cry. When I recovered I resolved to inform Mr Foster that I was *not* going to teach science. No way. I was going to put my foot down.

Feeling sorry for myself wasn't going to get me far, so I headed into the pub to grab a feed. The front bar was now packed. I ordered a middy. In front of me, stretching the length of the bar, was a photo of a cowboy leaning on the bar with his horse. That's right, his horse. The Royal was a 'watering hole'. I looked around half expecting everyone to be wearing six-shooters. They certainly had everything else. Hopalong Cassidy would have been proud of the hats these guys wore. They were big. Not just the hats but the men as well. It was like walking into a saloon in Dodge City.

I ordered a second middy. The barmaid, a vivacious lady who turned out to be the publican's wife, winked at me. I had no idea what this meant but I smiled pathetically. No one took the slightest notice of me. They were too busy celebrating the Tigers' latest thrashing. I soon found out where everyone had been; the Tenterfield Tigers had been playing a home game and the whole town had turned out to cheer them on. Everyone, it seems, except the high school principal. The fact they'd lost by a cricket score didn't affect the amount of booze that flowed in the front bar of The Royal.

The people in Tenterfield liked a drink. The first thing I learned about the town was that its population of 3000 was served by five pubs and two registered clubs, all doing a roaring trade. When you consider that at least 50 per cent of the population were women and children, you get an idea of the capacity of the locals. Not that the women didn't drink, it's just that most of them didn't frequent the front bar of The Royal, or any other front bar. It was 1973 and feminism hadn't made much of an impact in the Northern Table-lands. Yet.

The other thing I learned was that Tenterfield was a meatworks town. There were two meatworks that provided employment, one in Tenterfield and another across the border in Wallangarra. Many parents of the kids I would teach worked in one of the two meat-works. Many kids would end up there too when they left school.

The next day I woke up and decided I'd take the old man's advice and make the most of my predicament. I bounced out of bed, washed and combed my shoulder length hair and dressed in matching ensemble of mauve body shirt, wide maroon tie, beige shorts and long white socks. I rocked up to school and made my way to the front office. Once again I basked in the sensation of being the centre of attention as I made my way across the play-ground. Little did I know what that meant. The kids were checking me out all right – they were checking out their new target!

When I put my case to Mr Foster he patiently pointed out that a science teacher had just resigned and they had enough English teachers at present and he was in a bit of a pickle; he'd see what he could do but could I manage for a while? My first class was Year 9 science. (Back then we referred to classes as 'forms' not 'years'. I'm not sure when 'forms' became 'years' and even less sure why. Year 7 used to be First Form, Year 8 was Second Form, and so on. To make it easier for everyone under 50, I'll refer to forms as years.)

My memory of those first few lessons is blurry. I do remember a big strapping boy in my Year 8 woodwork class called Jake taking me under his wing. He was a bit like my *consigliere* although I was so far from being a mafia boss it wasn't funny. He was 14. I was 22. He told me to keep my head down, which I did. Jake had a droll sense of humour and a clear sense of right and wrong; he became my moral barometer and, later, a friend. Jake taught me a lot more than I taught him.

While Jake counselled me, Mr Wood, the head of manual arts – or whatever it was called then – considered me a feral pest. Come to think of it, most of the older members of staff seemed to look at me with undisguised suspicion or world-weary resignation. But Mr Wood's contempt was palpable. He thought I was 'up myself', which was probably true, and a 'fly-by-nighter' who would neither stick around nor amount to anything. I am indebted to him though; he did provide me with one of the best lines in a play I was to write many years later.

The staff, like most other staffs, were an eclectic bunch: some old, some young, some in between. The young were well and truly wet behind the ears, and there weren't many of us. The older ones were experienced in life and teaching. Most of them had settled in the town and several had farms. In my arrogant youth I thought many were only teaching to pay off the mortgage. They weren't educational crusaders like I was; they weren't in it to change the course of the nation's youth. They regarded teaching as a *job* and me as an upstart. I would soon find out why there weren't a lot of young teachers at Tenterfield.

At some point during that first day I put up my hand to coach the school's Rugby League team. I didn't know my way around, I didn't know anyone's name and I'd only ever played Rugby Union, but none of this fazed me. The 'offer' to coach the team came at a staff meeting and I recall the boss wearily asking for volunteers. The elders on the staff weren't too keen on volunteering for anything; they just wanted to get home to their farms and gardens and whatever else occupied their time. I can see now that it was a relief to the guy who rid himself of it, but at the time I took it as a wonderful opportunity to dive in and begin revolutionising the school. I remember someone pointing out that we'd be lucky to scratch up a team at all but that didn't worry me. Not only would we get a team together but we'd pull off the greatest upset in Rugby League history.

Told you I was up myself.

I survived the first day but by the second there was no hiding my ineptitude. My classes were a cue to riot. The kids loved them; the other teachers weren't so impressed. Mr Wood virtually banished me to back of the room. The head of science prayed I wouldn't blow up the lab. I didn't know how to quell a riot; I wasn't the type to grab a kid by the scruff of the neck, frog-march him into the store room and give him a thrashing. I wasn't into corporal punishment and getting belted certainly didn't make me behave when I was at school. There had to be another way. Could volunteering to coach the footy team serve as an antidote to the riots?

Word travelled fast at Tenterfield. The school had only 350 kids – possibly the smallest high school in the state. Pretty soon everyone knew that training was on and so, on my second night, at a new school and in a new town, I found myself coaching the school Rugby League team. We had a few experienced players, a couple of lively enthusiasts, and one or two who'd never laced on a boot. Jake, despite being in Year 8 and just 14, was not only one of our most experienced players, he was one of our best. We were about to play Moree in the University Shield, a state-wide, fiercely contested competition. Most teams were made up of 17- and 18-year-olds, and Moree was one of the toughest and best teams in the competition. It was going to be some game!

We had the bare minimum of 13 players; any injuries and we'd be in trouble. At this stage I had no idea what year these kids were even in, except for Jake. They were as keen as mustard though. And tough. I held out great hopes for an upset.

After training I returned to The Royal and, deciding it was a bit depressing in my room, made my way to the bar for a nightcap. I was pretty chirpy. All in all, things weren't going too badly.

The bar was packed. Tuesday night. The senior team had been training too. I got myself a beer and turned around to be greeted by two kids from my team. I nearly fell over. What were they doing in the pub? One of them had a squash and the other a beer.

'G'day, sir.'

What was I to do? Ignore them?

'Boys.'

It was a bit awkward. I shuffled from one foot to the other and wished the floor would swallow me up.

'Settlin' in okay?'

'Yes, thanks.'

Conversations often began like this in Tenterfield. Lots of subtext. There were plenty of silences as we nodded and smiled and smiled and nodded. Eventually we started to loosen up and they started asking me lots of questions, like where I came from and what university I went to. They were inquisitive. They seemed to want to know about the world outside Tenterfield. The conversation started to flow a little more easily.

'Beer?'

Nikolas had downed his beer and was offering me another. Here I was, a first-year-out teacher, still a kid myself, and I was getting into a shout with students. I had no idea of the protocols in a situation like this. It was all new to me, but I didn't feel I could turn my back on them. Besides, they were the most welcoming people I'd met, by a long chalk. Surely they were 18 and in Year 12 – how else could they be there? When Nik returned with the beers I decided it was my turn to lead off.

'So, what are you going to do after the HSC?' I asked.

'I'm in Year 9,' replied Philip, or 'Snowy' as everyone called him. Year 9! I nearly dropped my beer.

'Mum works in the kitchen.'

Talk about starting on the wrong foot! My second day on the job and I was drinking with a 14-year-old! Nowadays I'd be jailed. I'd be accused of child abuse, probably labelled a paedophile, and definitely run out of town. The phrase 'duty of care' hadn't been invented yet but I'm sure that drinking with your students would not be regarded as fulfilling it!

I scraped my jaw off the floor and asked Nik what year he was in.

'Year 10.'

It was so matter-of-fact. They were unfazed. Totally unfazed. Of course, I freaked out; I got out of there as quickly as I could. I didn't even finish my beer.

When I ran into the two kids at school the next day, it was as if the whole thing had either been a mirage or of no significance. It was never mentioned. We said hello and got on with our day.

This was the beginning of my practical education at Tenterfield.

First period

My Dip. Ed. had been fun and interesting but in no way did it prepare me for what I was about to experience in the world of teaching. Especially the world of teaching in a small country town.

We'd studied lots of theory, some of it quite radical. Jean Piaget's *Psychology and Epistemology: Towards a Theory of Knowledge*, Jean-Jacques Rousseau's *The Social Contract*, Everett Reimer's *School is Dead: Alternatives in Education*, and of course, the bible, AS Neill's *Summerhill*. These works affected the way I looked at kids. I never saw them as the enemy, I never saw the classroom as a battlefield. I never embraced the hierarchical structure that still besets the school system. I always valued, and perhaps overvalued, kids' opinions. That isn't to say I was a believer in 'alternative' education where the kids could do as they please. I accepted the need for boundaries and I wasn't about to let the kids in my care walk all over me. Oh no.

One of the last lectures we received in our Dip. Ed. had been delivered by a stern-faced department official. It was a kind of pep talk before we went out into the real world of teaching. He virtually told us to forget everything we'd learnt, to keep our heads down and do as we were told. All that theory was just that: theory.

'Don't think you're going to change anything.'

I couldn't believe my ears. Who was he kidding? The world

was turning upside down and we were meant to carry on as though nothing was happening. If schools and their teachers didn't reflect the world around them, then how could they be of any possible relevance to the kids who attended them? And what was the point of all that theory if we were just going to ignore the lessons we'd learnt? One thing was for certain, I wasn't going to maintain the status quo, even if I didn't know how to control a class.

I battled along that first week in a daze. I didn't do any 'teaching' – I was more like an ineffectual member of the riot police. I was holding the fort, waiting for my big break as an English/ history teacher. The footy team was my only salvation.

On Monday morning Mr Foster called me into his office. I thought I must have done something wrong. Maybe I was in trouble. Maybe he'd found out about my drinking with Year 9s and 10s …

'I've got good news for you.'

I've been transferred back to Gunnedah?

'Miss Black has resigned. You're the new English/history teacher. Report to Mr Lamb.'

I nearly jumped out of my skin. Here it was, the moment I'd been waiting for. My own timetable. My own classes. My chance to change the world. I was too excited to ask about Miss Black. One day she was there, the next she was gone. No explanation why. All I knew was that I was the grateful beneficiary of her premature departure.

I headed up to the English/history staff room to meet Mr Lamb. A large, avuncular man, Mr Lamb was born and bred in the town. He'd been a pilot in World War II and was a bit of a local identity: President of the Golf Club, President of Rotary. He showed me to my desk, my own desk – it was such a grown-up moment! The desk was almost pristine. Miss Black had cleared out all her belongings and disappeared into thin air.

Mr Lamb handed me my timetable and introduced me to the rest of the staff. They all seemed preoccupied. A few nods, a couple of handshakes, they were all too busy preparing for the day to have much time for me. Staff rooms were a hive of activity on Monday mornings. Everyone was working out how they were going to survive the oncoming week, planning lessons on the hop and wondering how to deal with the weekend's hangover and that uncontrollable Year 8 class. I looked at my timetable. I was on first period. That was ten minutes away. What'll I do? Mr Lamb handed me a key and, before I could ask what it was for, left me to it.

One of my new colleagues, Miss Eliot, pointed at the key as she gave me a handout.

'That's for the classroom.'

I looked at the handout. It was a poem. John Donne.

'Most of them have probably lost it. I'd run off a few extras if I were you.'

'Thanks.'

Along with Mr Lamb, Miss Eliot belonged to the older camp. She too was born in the town and, like Mr Lamb, was also single. She was slightly eccentric in a *Prime of Miss Jean Brodie* way. She was a brilliant teacher and, once my eyes were opened, she taught me a lot. She was also passionate about cricket; every year she made a pilgrimage to the Sydney Cricket Ground to watch the Test series. When I made this discovery down the track, we bonded further. But just now, on the cusp of my teaching debut, I was way too self-absorbed to give her a second thought.

I grabbed the John Donne poem and raced off to the Gestetner machine. This was a time before photocopying became universal. It was a time when computers were the size of small buildings. Laptops were a fantasy; email and the internet a distant dream.

I pushed my way in and asked someone to show me how to use the machine. They were too busy. Fortunately Julie came rushing in. She was late. She'd go away every weekend to visit her boy-friend and was late every Monday morning. My desk was next to hers. She was my age and we became quite good friends. She saw my dilemma.

'You got 3E2?'

3E2 were a Year 9 class.

'Yeah, I ...'

She raised her eyebrows and grabbed the handout from me.

'I'll run off some extra copies off for you.'

'Thanks.'

'3E2 are a bit of a handful.'

I smiled. 'Thanks.'

But I didn't need any advice. I was supremely confident. After all, I was teaching my subject area now. They'd be fine.

The Gestetner whirred into action. Whenever I used it I ended up with ink all over my hands. I soon discovered that if I wanted to hand work out I needed to get it to the office staff well in advance so they could run it off for me – a lesson I never learnt very well. Julie handed me the copies with their distinctive smell of fresh ink and wished me luck.

I raced upstairs, grabbed my roll and key and sprinted towards the classroom. The bell rang and the whole school began lining up in their years: Monday morning assembly. This gave me a bit of breathing space to dream up creative ways of teaching poetry.

My first assembly at Tenterfield was like every other assembly I've attended. The deputy reminded everyone about putting rub-bish in bins, taking pride in the school and, inevitably, finished off with something about school uniforms. The boss was suitably stern, praising the school's sporting/cultural/academic achievements and damning the boys' boorish behaviour on whatever public transport was relevant to the area. The PE teacher made sporting announce-ments and other members of staff talked up their pet projects. A few earnest teachers paraded up and down, giving out warnings and sending ratbags to the office. Any ambitious young teacher worth their salt saw this as a perfect opportunity to display their disciplinary skills to anyone who might notice, while the rest of the staff surreptitiously discussed the weekend's socialising or the latest political crisis, or dreamt of Friday afternoon.

Most kids were respectfully disengaged during assembly. They stood or sat, as the case may be, patiently. It was a ritual they quietly endured. They thought about their weekends or the boy/girl they had a crush on, or suddenly remembered the homework they hadn't done. Their faces were mostly vacant as the speakers droned on through the scratchy PA system. Sometimes a guest speaker would struggle with the PA or consider this an opportunity to display their non-existent oratory skills. ANZAC Day ceremonies were particularly memorable in this regard and some well-meaning old digger would be trotted out to raise the flag as *The Last Post* was 'played'. About the only time the kids sparked into life was when one of their number addressed the assembly. As soon as a kid took the PA the rest of assembly became decidedly animated. I think there might have been a lesson in this.

On this day a couple of miscreants were hauled out and sent to the office. They became instant celebrities and didn't seem to display much contrition. They were hardly shuddering in their boots as they made their way, wrestling with each other, across the playground.

At Tenterfield the conclusion of these formalities signalled a kind of free-for-all. The theory was that we'd gather up our charges and march them off to class. The reality was that kids would hang around, swap yarns and wander off to class when they were good and ready.

There were two Year 9 classes, 3E1 and 3E2. They were streamed and 3E2 wasn't the top class. One thing I discovered pretty quickly was that Mr Lamb (and many other head teachers I served under) had a habit of allocating all the difficult classes to the young, first-year-out teachers. He kept the best ones for himself. Miss Eliot got the next best and so on down the line in order of seniority. As I was the most recent arrival, the most junior of the juniors, I got the 'bottom' classes.

The two boys who had been hauled out of assembly were in 3E2. They would be late. I was given this information by Candy, one of the girls who had taken it upon herself to show me the ropes.

'Brumby and Freddo gotta go to the deputy's.'

I thanked her, even though I had no idea who she was talking about.

'You the new teacher?'

'Yes.'

She laughed. The other girls giggled. The boys paid me no attention whatsoever. They were too busy pushing and shoving and tripping each other up.

'This way.'

Candy was a nice girl. She was being helpful and I was grateful.

Our classroom was in an old weatherboard building with a veranda out the front. I hardly noticed the wood-fired heater in the corner until winter. I soon discovered its value and learnt to keep the fire stoked to ward off the cold. The whole building had a slightly rustic, frontier feel to it, like *Little House on the Prairie*. On one side of the classroom the windows opened onto the veranda, the other side onto High Street. In the early days I wasted a lot of time telling kids not to look out the window – as if what was going on outside could be more interesting than my lesson! But kids looking out the window would prove to be the least of my concerns.

The kids were sort of lined up waiting for me to unlock the

door. I pushed my way through and obliged. The desks were neatly arranged in rows. The blackboard was spotless. I took a moment to take it in. It was only a moment because I was nearly bowled over by the stampede. The boys were rushing for pole position along the back row. Minor scuffles broke out as they fought for their seats. Within seconds the room was a disaster area. Bags everywhere, desks out of line, chairs tipped over.

'Sit down everybody.'

I was being warm and friendly.

'Please sit down.'

No one took the slightest notice of me. They were too busy catching up on the gossip or taking the piss out of each other, or both. Then it hit me. I was alone. In front of my own class. For the first time. These were unchartered waters. There was no back up; there wasn't even a class next door with another member of staff to call on if things got out of hand. And things were quickly getting out of hand. This wasn't how I'd envisaged it. No one seemed to behave like this when I was prac teaching or at Gunnedah. For some reason I assumed that when I got to teach the subjects I'd be trained to teach, all would fall into place. Nothing could have been further from the truth. The kids were onto me from the start. They knew I was easy pickings. There's not much you can hide from kids, no matter how much you pretend.

I took refuge behind the desk and waited. And prayed. There was no point in shouting. I knew that instinctively. I wasn't much of a shouter anyway.

Eventually order was restored, although it had nothing to do with me. The kids sorted it out. They knew the pecking order; they knew who should sit where. I was an innocent bystander. Most of the girls sat down the front and grinned at me. I immediately got the sense that these girls were going to chew me up and spit me out. Beside them sat a few 'conchs' (conscientious or, more accurately in 3E2, vaguely motivated students). The 'try-hard' naughty kids got the middle. The dreamers naturally gravitated to the windows. The 'ratbags' leaned their chairs against the back wall on two legs, just the way I used to. My own behaviour at school was coming back to bite me. Karma.

I noticed that two places up the back had been left empty. A knock at the door ... Brumby and Freddo sauntered in and took their places behind the vacant desks up the back. They might have given me some cursory acknowledgement, but the reality was that they were the seasoned players, I was the debutant. Whatever punishment had been metered out to them was water off a duck's back and only served to raise their already lofty status among their peer group. They settled into a well-rehearsed, suitably insolent position, leaning back against the wall and silently challenging me to do my best. The rest of the class looked at them and then looked at me. I was up to it.

'Good morning 3E2. My name is Mr Manning.'

So?

I looked at the sea of faces before me. Each one told a story; some already had a history etched on them. There wasn't a lot of innocence out there. The most innocent person in that room was standing out the front. Suddenly I realised that Snowy was there. He didn't draw attention to himself or make any reference to the fact we'd been out drinking together. He was quite neutral. He was way cooler than I was.

There was a moment's silence. They were all waiting for my next move.

'I'm your new teacher.'

So far so good.

'I look forward to getting to know you.'

Really?

'I've got a few rules ...'

Oh yeah?

I ploughed on.

'Hands up if you want to ask a question. No talking when someone else is talking. Um ...'

I noticed my mouth was dry. I swallowed. And smiled pathetically.

'Now if you don't mind, I'd better call the roll.'

The thought of telling the boys up the back to sit properly flitted across my mind but I decided to keep my powder dry.

I started calling the roll. Hands were raised. Grunts were grunted. A couple might have said 'Here' or 'Sir'. Whatever they did, presence was being accounted for and absence was noted. About halfway through Freddo called out:

'Where's Miss Black?'

He smirked. He knew where she was. He'd been part of the reason she'd left. He also hadn't put his hand up. Was I going to challenge him? Take him on? For the second time in less than a minute I dodged it.

'I don't know.'

'How long you gunna last?'

'Pardon?'

'We got ridda three already.'

General hilarity.

The ship was slipping away. I could feel it heading down the slipway before I'd even launched it. The champagne was still on ice and already a mutiny was brewing.

If there were 'high fives' in those days, there would have been high-fiveing all over the place. They were celebrating the fact that they'd driven another young teacher out of the school. What they didn't know was that they'd probably driven her out of teaching altogether.

'Please. Settle down.'

Conversations sparked up like spot fires, witty anecdotes about the dismembering of Miss Black. I didn't even know what she looked like but I was already empathising with her.

'Quiet!'

I was pissing in the wind. Then one of my allies in the front row piped up.

'Shut up you guys. Give him a go.'

The boys returned fire.

'Sure, Candy.'

'Randy Candy.'

Hilarious.

Candy responded by throwing a pen.

'Fuck off.'

I pretended not to hear this and battled on.

'Renouf, Smith, Tate …'

Somehow I got to the end.

'Woolley.'

I was exhausted. Already. It felt like I'd been in that classroom for an hour. It'd been less than ten minutes. Thirty-five minutes and 17 seconds to go. I didn't know how I was going to make it. I was learning about the contrary nature of time: it raced when things were going well, it stopped dead in its tracks when things were going badly. And right now it was like the spring in my watch had unravelled, not to mention the spring in my step. The minute hand had stopped dead. The bloody watch wasn't working! I was freaking out. I wanted to run out the door, jump in my car and disappear down the New England Highway. But I couldn't, I couldn't let this mob beat me.

'It's going to take me a bit of time to learn your names.'

But some names went straight in: Brumby, Freddo, Candy, Snowy … They were already chiselled into my subconscious. Others would take longer and some I would never learn. Still others I would develop a weird dyslexia with. I don't know why but some names I just kept on forgetting or mispronouncing. There was no rhyme or reason to this, and some of those whose names I constantly mispronounced were kids I really liked. It wasn't to do with ethnicity, it was just the way my brain worked.

Of course, over a 40-year teaching career I learnt a lot of names. Hundreds, even thousands of them. It's funny when you're walking down the street and someone catches your eye and there's a sudden spark of recognition.

'Mr Manning!'

I'm staring at a six-foot-six giant with a beard and hair halfway down his back. He's covered in tats and has a skull and crossbones hanging from his earlobes.

'You remember me? You taught me in Year 7.'

'Of course …'

'Simon.'

'Yes, Simon. I know.'

'You forgot my name.'

He's hurt. Maybe he's going to flatten me.

'No …'

'Tenterfield 1973.'

'I remember you, Simon. How could I forget?' How could I …

Meanwhile back in class, and facing impending disaster, I decided I had nothing to lose.

'Please take out your books.'

My confidence had taken an early battering but I knew I could come back. I was like one of those toys at the Show that gets knocked down but keeps bouncing back up. To my eternal relief they took out their books – or at least some of them did. I suspect Snowy had something to do with encouraging those in his immediate vicinity to give me a go. The girls in the front row were keen to please. Mary was especially keen. She didn't think she should be in 3E2 and I was her ticket out of there. I'm not sure why she thought that, but she did. Mary came from across the border in Wallangarra; I thought Tenterfield was small, but I soon learnt it was a metropolis compared to Wallangarra. Mary was one of those kids who was going to make it no matter what obstacles were put in front of her. She wanted to learn. She wanted to do well. And she did.

'Today we're going to do some poetry.'

Eyes rolled back in heads and groans emanated from the back row. During assembly I'd decided that John Donne was too conventional for me. I was going to blow them out of the water with something way more hip and groovy. I'd get them to write their own poems. I wrote on the board:

The poet is not a special kind of man, but every man is a special kind of poet.

I should have changed *man* to *person* but this was only the dawn of feminism. We all had a lot to learn.

'Please copy this down.'

It was the sort of quote that underpinned everything I did at Tenterfield. I was on a mission to make everyone feel they were 'special'. It was the basis of my education philosophy, if I had one. I was convinced that every kid could be a star in whatever they did. I was convinced that we would beat Moree in the footy; even if we were trailing 50–0, we could still come back. I was convinced that Mary would be a Rhodes Scholar and that 3E2 would become the best young poets in the world. Of course, some of this derived from my own inflated ego and my confidence rather grated on the more experienced members of staff.

'I'd like you to write a short verse.'

'Poetry?'

'Us?'

'Yes. Keep it simple. Write about an animal, a fish, a plant or a place. Be specific. Small details … like this.'

I turned to write on the board:

Silky, slinky
Slithering silently,
Stepping softly,
Proud and dignified,
Black and beautiful.   — *LW Canada*

Cue riot.

I thought I had them in the palm of my hand but I never had them anywhere; they were just taking a breather. As soon as I turned away, all hell broke loose and 3E2 set about demonstrating exactly how they'd got rid of three teachers in six weeks. Pens became darts. Rulers transformed into swords. Bags, shields. Chairs, missiles. Desks, barricades. Paper aeroplanes filled the air. What were they doing? This wasn't a history lesson. We weren't re-creating the Battle of Britain, but it was the Battle of 3E2. It was mayhem. It was like I'd flicked a switch. Was it the poetry? Was it writing? Was it me?

No. It was business as usual on Monday morning at Tenterfield High School in 1973. I did my best to bring peace but I was about as effective as appeasement had been. The fact was, even though I was the teacher, I had no authority at all, not over these guys. I was like the boy on the burning deck:

Upon his brow he felt their breath,
And in his waving hair,
And looked from that lone post of death,
In still yet brave despair …

Mary tried to ask a question but I could hardly hear her for the racket. And it was building. I was worried that someone would come in and complain about it. They must have heard it across the playground in the main building. Everyone on High Street would have heard it. Everyone at Tenterfield would be looking, wondering what the hell was going on. I was worried I'd be found out, exposed as a fraud.

I'd like to think I jumped up and down in an effort to bring them to order but the truth is I didn't even do that. I just stood there staring into the abyss. I didn't know what to do. I was a boy in a man's world except the men were seven years younger than me. If time had stood still before, it had atrophied now. I had never known anything like this feeling. Utter helplessness. Total inadequacy. If I was a tough guy I might have grabbed someone by the scruff of the neck and tossed him out the window. But I was as tough as a marshmallow. I was so exposed I might as well have been stark naked. No wonder some of the girls took pity on me.

Mary had seen enough of this – she was there to learn. She took over.

'Why don't you send them out?'

That's a good idea. Why didn't I think of that? I remembered that I could send someone to the head teacher, but it was meant to be a last resort, not something you'd resort to halfway through your first lesson. It would be a terrible admission of my inadequacy as a teacher. It would be well and truly running up the white flag. It would send a clear signal to the kids that they had me where they wanted me.

'If you don't stop that ...'

'What?'

'Did you hear me?'

No. How could they? I could hardly hear myself.

'Sit down. Get back to your seat!!'

A window was thrown open and a bag flew out.

'Who threw that bag out the window?'

'He did.'

'She did.'

'I did not.'

'Then who did?'

It was hopeless. It was a circus. Nothing I tried had any impact whatsoever. These were highly charged, testosterone-fuelled adolescents on overdrive and I was a helpless, middle-class 22-year-old trying to assert my non-existent authority. I couldn't understand what was going on and I couldn't understand why. What had I done wrong? I was being friendly, I was trying to give them the benefit of my wisdom …

'I'm going to have to send someone out!'

They were quaking in their boots. I repeated my threat. I had to do something to assert my authority.

'You. Out!'

A boy up the back who was built like a lumberjack looked at me.

'What did I do?'

'You threw that … didn't you?'

'Who says?'

This was a confrontation. Me and the lumberjack. *The Gunfight at the OK Corral*. I'd made an accusation and I'd better be right. Was I sure it was him? No. He was just – I don't know – in the neighbourhood. I mustered up every bit of gravitas I could.

'Sit down.'

He didn't actually tell me to 'fuck off' but there wasn't much in it.

'I said sit down!'

He looked at me as though I were invisible. But I wasn't going to let him get on top of me. Oh no. I was going to … I was …

'Please. Sit down.'

I was virtually on my knees. I could feel my face going red. The room fell silent. The rest of the class could smell blood. The chorus of girls up the front were on the edge of their seats. Everyone else looked on. It must have been great theatre. Was this going to be the record? A teacher dismissed before the end of his first lesson? Hold the presses.

No one had prepared me for this moment. No lecturer had taught us to deal with this. It hadn't appeared in the edition of AS Neil's *Summerhill* that I'd devoured at university. This was hand-to-hand combat with a 15-year-old and, if bets were laid, the 15-year-old would have been the odds-on favourite. I could turn and run or I could fight for my dignity. I chose the latter.

'Out!'

The lumberjack looked at me. I was pointing to the door. I was putting my foot down.

'I've had enough ...'

'What'd I do?'

'Go and report to Mr Lamb.'

He could tell I was serious. He picked up his bag, gave another boy a clip over the ear and casually wandered out. He was almost laughing.

'Want me to shut the door?'

'Thanks. You know where to go?'

What a silly question – this kid could find his way to the office blindfolded.

If I thought this display of disciplinary clout would have an effect on the rest of the class, I was sadly mistaken. I had clearly shown that I had no control. I was a pushover. They were quiet for a couple of seconds, then someone did something to someone else and it was on again.

'Don't!'

'What?'

'It's mine.'

'Who says?'

'You took it ...'

'Did not.'

I put my foot down: 'Don't think I won't send another ...'

The victim of whatever transgression had taken place took the law into his own hands and pushed the other boy over. I wasn't going to stand for this kind of behaviour.

'You. Out!'

Another one bit the dust. He picked up his bag and gave the rest of the class the 'V'. I think this was a 'V' for 'victory' and not 'up yours'. His fans cheered. He strolled out after the lumberjack, grinning as he went. I felt I'd shrunk to the size of a gnat. They were toying with me. They were daring me to throw them out – all of them. I'd lost the battle and now I was rapidly losing the war. How was this going to end? With the whole class in Mr Lamb's office?

Eventually peace was restored, I can't remember exactly how. Clearly I wasn't a challenge for 3E2. They'd wiped the floor with me and were perhaps bored with playing run-over-the-teacher. What I do remember is that we had a lesson of sorts. They wrote some poetry and some of it was pretty good. The moment Mary read hers I leapt on it as if she were a young Oodgeroo Noonuccal (Kath Walker). 'Positive reinforcement' isn't the half of it. Snowy took pity on me and read out his poem. Others followed. They were great – I couldn't praise them enough. I was flying. Fortunately, Freddo and Brumby were having a nap. Sleeping off a big weekend. Or maybe saving themselves …

The bell rang.

'Here endeth the lesson.'

Thank God. I had survived. I was on cloud nine.

'See ya, sir.'

I'd nailed it. I'd won them over. A couple even gestured goodbye as they pushed their way out the door. Mary asked me a question about poetry. I was stoked.

I was also exhausted. I felt like I'd gone ten rounds with a revolving door. Was this the traditional 'softening up' period, like in league games at the time when both teams spent the first ten minutes bashing each other up before settling down to play?

I hoped so. I hoped they would be gentler with me next time. I was pretty sure there was nothing malicious about these kids. And I was right.

When I got back to the staff room Mr Lamb reminded me that sending kids out was a last resort.

Classroom control?

I had a free period so I sat down and began preparing for the next lesson: 2E3, a Year 8 class. I tried to work out what Miss Black had done with them. I looked up the register, which is where we were meant to record what we'd taught. It was empty. It didn't take long to find out why.

If I thought 3E2 had been tough I was in for a rude awakening when I met 2E3. They were simply out of control. They had no interest in school. Most of them would take advantage of the law that said you could leave school at 14-and-a-half. The moment that date arrived they'd be out the door and onto a horse or into the boning room at the meatworks or, in some cases, off to the maternity ward. Needless to say 2E3 had me for breakfast.

A quirk of timetabling meant that on Wednesdays I had 2E3 first and third period. First period was usually vaguely manageable. Then I had a 'break' with 3E2. Then 2E3 would return for more. Those mornings were a nightmare, and I'm not using the term 'nightmare' loosely. I have no idea how I got through to recess. Every Wednesday I dragged myself across the playground and struggled up to the staffroom where I devoured half-a-dozen Monte Carlos and gulped down a bucket of tea in an effort to calm my nerves. It didn't work. I was like a soldier in World War I returning to the trenches after an incursion into enemy territory.

I was shell-shocked, my nerves were jangled, I was a mess. Once I'd regained whatever composure I could muster I'd be confronted with the thought that in a week's time I'd have to do it all over again. The enemy would be there every Wednesday, howitzers aimed directly at me, ready to blow me to smithereens. My chances of survival weren't high.

There was one saving grace and it came in the shape of a Year 10 class, 4E1. Initially I wasn't meant to teach 4E1 – they were way too good a class for a novice like me. They were in the capable hands of Miss Eliot. I think she must have taken pity on me because there was some kind of timetable reshuffle and I was given 4E1. Miss Eliot's generosity saved my life.

My first lesson with 4E1 was a real eye-opener. Miss Eliot had given them a good rap but I still approached them with a fair amount of caution. I took a deep breath, walked in and introduced myself. No one threw anything, at me or anyone else. They were remarkably civilised, almost polite. They sat up and waited. Unbelievably, they seemed to be interested in what I had to say. It was unreal! I fell in love with them immediately. I would almost run to their classes. When attempting to quell a riot in 2E3, I would comfort myself with the thought that there was light at the end of the tunnel: 4E1.

Having a class I could relate to changed the whole ball game. I didn't have to waste time on crowd control; I could get straight into it. 4E1 wanted to know about the world at large and I was more than happy to introduce them to it. I wanted to teach and they gave me permission. They were enough to keep the flame alive. They restored my faith and my self-esteem.

Those first few weeks at Tenterfield were an introduction to the vagaries of full-time teaching as well as a lesson in life. I was see-sawing between incredible highs and appalling lows. One afternoon as I was driving home I saw a group of boys standing outside the Paragon Cafe. They were in 3E2. I waved to them. They gave me 'the bird'. I nearly ran off the road. I thought I was getting somewhere with them. I thought we were connecting. That 'finger' was devastating. It was worse than any riot; it was a personal slap in the face. It told me that I was deluding myself. I went home, collapsed and wept tears of frustration. It was 3.30 in the afternoon.

That single gesture was the worst thing I'd ever experienced. I'd invested so much in that class. I'd been determined to turn them around and, subconsciously, I'd believed I could. If someone in 4E1 had done that to me I would probably have thrown myself off Bluff Rock.

The next day I pulled myself together and went back to face the music. I had 3E2 first. I'm not sure what I was expecting but the boys had forgotten all about the incident. It hadn't meant anywhere near as much to them as it had to me. That was a lesson in itself.

So too was the day I walked into 2E3 to find 'Woody' Forrester strung up on the exposed beams of the ceiling. A group of kids, including Jake, the boy who'd protected me during the first week, were standing around laughing and admiring their handiwork. Woody was hanging in the air like some large animal being winched from a natural disaster by helicopter. They'd roped his upper and lower torso to the beams so his arms and legs were dangling down. It was quite comical. I decided to make light of it. I'd already learnt from bitter experience that going in hard was a complete waste of time.

'Hey Woody, what are you doing up there?'

Jake fixed me with one of his famous 'steady gazes'. You don't mess with Jake when he looks at you like that. Eyeball to eyeball.

'He's got a handle.'

'What?'

'You heard me.'

I'd blown it. I'd tried to be cool, tried to be 'one of the boys' and curry favour by joining in on the joke and using a nickname. It hadn't cut the mustard. Not with Jake.

'Show some respect. Use his handle.'

'Sorry Jake. Would you guys mind getting Stephen down?'

His 'handle' was Stephen. I hadn't earned the right to call him Woody. That was important; the fact that they'd roped him to the roof was almost incidental. This was about respect. They let Stephen down and we got on with the lesson.

That 2E3 class had its fair share of characters, such as Tommy Thompson and Rowdy Callahan. They were tough. Really tough. They lived somewhere in the mountains. They rode their horses to the bus stop and caught feral animals to amuse themselves while they waited for it to arrive. They often let wild cats loose in the playground just to stir things up a bit. You didn't argue with Tommy and Rowdy. Or I didn't. I would try to navigate them towards the end of the lesson by any means possible. I didn't care if they didn't do any work, and it wouldn't have mattered if I did. They pretty much did as they pleased. As far as I was concerned, as long as I got through the lesson reasonably intact, I was happy.

On Fridays I would read 2E3 a story for last period. They were pretty chilled by this stage; they'd created havoc all week and were resting up for Friday night and whatever the weekend would hold. While they were taking a breather I'd be praying to get to the bell without a disaster breaking out. On one particular day half the class were asleep and the rest were looking out the window. Rowdy was sitting in the front row next to Betty Bloomfield. Betty was a pleasant girl but you wouldn't want to cross her. As I read them *The Adventures of Tom Sawyer* I secretly congratulated myself on the fact that Rowdy wasn't causing any trouble. He was quiet for the first time ever and it was nice. Even pleasant.

I enjoyed reading to classes. I probably liked the sound of my own voice. As I paused at an appropriately dramatic moment I peered over the book to see Betty smiling weirdly. Rowdy was smiling too, a kind of self-satisfied smile right in front of me. Something was a bit odd. I read on. When I paused again and looked up I saw that Rowdy had his hand in Betty's pants. He was leaning back staring straight at me. Betty's eyes were rolling back in her head. She could have been anywhere. This wasn't in the *Teaching Manual*. It certainly wasn't something we'd been warned about during the Dip. Ed. The rest of the class were oblivious to these carnal goings-on; they were waiting for the bell. So was I. Was Rowdy challenging me? Or was he just … being Rowdy? I couldn't send them out, nor could I say, 'Stop fingering that girl!' I hadn't the faintest idea what to do. I returned to *Tom Sawyer*.

'I ain't doing my duty by that boy, and that's the Lord's truth, goodness knows. Spare the rod and spile the child, as the Good Book says.'

I'm sure my voice faltered. I couldn't look in the direction of the illicit behaviour but I couldn't avoid it either. It was happening right under my nose. I felt myself going red. I tried to focus on Mark Twain's words but they'd gone all blurry. The time thing kicked in and the clock stood still. Betty was almost groaning. No, she *was* groaning. Rowdy was grinning like the cat who'd swallowed the you-know-what and I was wishing I had an invisibility cloak and could pass through the walls and disappear into the wide blue yonder.

At last the bell rang. I had to say something – I was the teacher, the moral guardian. I closed *Tom Sawyer* and wished 2E3 a pleasant weekend. Rowdy was walking towards me. He was waiting for a comment.

'There's a time and place for everything, Rowdy.'

'What?'

'Let's just leave it at that.'

'I didn't do nothing. I was good.'

'Have a good weekend, Rowdy.'

I didn't tell anyone about this incident, I was way too embarrassed. And who was I going to tell? Mr Lamb wouldn't have wanted to know about it. It was the sort of thing that made me grow up pretty fast.

I never really learnt to deal with Rowdy and Tommy. I don't think I taught them anything either. They were laws unto themselves, although they did make me laugh at times. On one occasion we hosted an inter-school basketball tournament and there were a hundred or so girls in the old Agricultural Hall, which doubled as a court. The girls were cheering wildly and getting into the game when the boys decided they'd ramp up the hysteria. They'd done some 'hunting' on the way to school and, having locked the hall from the outside, fed a 12-foot rock python in through the window.

The place exploded. Someone managed to open the door and release the crowd of screaming 14-year-old girls into the park. My last memory of the incident is of Tommy madly chasing them across the park with the python.

The thing is, I had no training to deal with these situations. Had anyone? It was more than just moving beyond my comfort zone; I was dealing with kids who had seen more and done more than I'd ever dreamt of. Take, for example, the girls in 3E2 who had taken to sitting in the front row, hitching up their already very short skirts and giving me an eyeful. At first I thought it might have been accidental; then I realised they were baiting me. It was deliberate and it went on for a year. They were toying with the naïve teacher who knew nothing about life. I don't think there was anything sexual in it – it was more a kind of game. But it was pretty unnerving, particularly when one of them brought her work up to my desk to be marked and started rubbing her crotch on my elbow. It took me a while to realise what she was doing. When I did, I froze. Again it was one of those situations that an inexperienced teacher could find himself in but which an experienced teacher might see coming and avoid.

I was young. Like many men in their early twenties, I masked self-doubt with a cloak of bravado, especially when I was dealing with the opposite sex. My initial reaction to these girls who were teasing me was to brand them little tarts. I'd never had anything to do with girls like them. I was totally ill-equipped to deal with young, feisty teenage girls, hell-bent on testing boundaries.

What is more, as a young male teacher I was often flattered by the attention these girls gave me. What young guy wouldn't be flattered by a pretty girl flirting with him? For that matter, what young female teacher wouldn't be flattered by a handsome young boy flirting with her? Or what young gay teacher of either sex wouldn't be flattered by the attention of a gay student? Flirting is part of life.

Young students flirt with young teachers, and vice versa. *Flirt* – nothing more. No amount of child protection legislation is going to stop it happening. Legislation can't stop a lot of things that go on in schools because schools are populated by human beings. But young teachers should be aware of the danger of responding to flirting and they should also know it's going to happen.

What's really scary is when you see an older teacher responding to this kind of behaviour. Weirdly some kids seem to flirt as a kind of default position. They're invariably good-looking. I'm not talking about kids with histories of child abuse, I'm talking about 'normal' kids who flirt. Most teachers learn to ignore this. Sadly some don't – they feed off it and it's not only incredibly inappropriate, it's incredibly sad and the kids lose all respect for the teacher in question. They become the butt of playground mockery.

Over time I learnt that kids often try out their newly discovered sexuality without even knowing they're doing it. I learnt to ignore it and to never place myself in a position where I could be compromised. I would never let a girl get as close to me as the girl whose work I was marking that day in Tenterfield. But of course she would never have tried that on with an older, more experienced teacher whom she knew wouldn't respond. She picked her mark way more astutely.

Extra-curricular

In Tenterfield I was oblivious to all this. I was trying to stay afloat and in doing so made some terrible misjudgements. The girls in the front row of 3E2 were a perfect case in point. What I didn't know about them was that they spent their mornings getting their little brothers and sisters off to school and had done a day's work around the house before I even got out of bed. School was downtime for them. They were back on duty after school, cooking dinner, putting siblings to bed, dealing with struggling parents. No wonder they had some fun with the git in the mauve body shirt!

Being in a small country town meant that, unless you hibernated in a cave, you had contact with the kids outside class time. You saw them up the street or in the shops or at the pool. You came to know their parents in a way you could never do in the city. You had dinner at their houses. By the time they were in Years 11 and 12 you went to the same parties. The boundaries were well and truly muddied by your proximity to the kids you taught.

I finally moved out of The Royal and into Stone Age, an old stone cottage that deserved to be heritage listed. There was a very thin wall dividing our half of Stone Age from our neighbours. Not much went on next door that you didn't bear witness to. This was often mildly amusing, as the couple next door had an active sex life. On the flip side they also had a tempestuous relationship and weren't afraid to trade blows when making a point. Their daughter, who was in one of my classes, was not immune to this. We would frequently exchange nods in the morning as we set off for school. More than once she was sporting bruises.

I soon leant that there wasn't much you could keep from the kids. After one pretty wild weekend I turned up to class to find all 3E2 grinning at me. A hand shot up.

'Have a good weekend, sir?'

'Yes ... thank you.'

'How was the shower?'

I went red. They laughed. They knew more about what I'd been up to than I did.

When I childishly lined a row of empty beer cans on the roof of a colleague's car, he was sent abusive letters by the townsfolk and nearly run out of town for setting a bad example. The irony was staggering, let alone the fact that he would hardly stack empty cans on the roof of his own car!

With a mixture of good fortune and bloody-minded determination I managed to survive those first few weeks at Tenterfield. One thing was for sure, no matter how much shit was thrown at me I was not going to give up. I was not going to follow Miss Black down the New England Highway. The kids were rough and tough but once they got to know you they loosened up – they didn't stop creating havoc, but they became more trusting.

The key to my survival was getting to know them outside class time. I took to extra-curricular activities like a duck to water. I had no choice, it was either drink myself to death or get involved in the life of the town. I coached teams, I played every sport imaginable, I staged plays, I played in a band (very badly). I did anything and everything. Kids were involved in all these activities; if you did anything in Tenterfield, you got to know the kids. This would never happen in a city school. The obvious pitfall was that the kids got to know you too, more perhaps than you might like. But it was a small price to pay.

Sport played a big role in my life as a teacher at Tenterfield. After we were summarily flogged by Moree in the University Shield I decided to coach a junior team. I had long-term plans for revenge but they never amounted to anything, of course. In those days there was regular Wednesday afternoon sport for all years, which, for me, was a godsend as it meant that I could meet the kids in a different context. It also meant that for a relatively isolated school like Tenterfield you could organise inter-school visits to Glen Innes and Guyra and even further afield to Gunnedah and Tamworth.

My junior team trained after school. The only way this could be managed was if I drove half the team home after training. The school bus left straight after school and without it there was no means of transport to outlying areas. So after training I would load up the VW and begin the circuit to the various drop-off points. The round trip took about an hour. Apart from the obvious advantage of keeping me out of the pub, it also enabled me to see another side to my charges. I saw where they lived. I came to understand the nature of their personal challenges. We talked endlessly about football and health and training and ambitions. We had a lot of laughs. Far from being a burden, these trips were liberating and fun.

Of course today you'd have to fill out a hundred risk-assessment forms and amass so many permission notes that driving kids home has become prohibitive. Not to mention the small matter of piling half-a-dozen kids into a VW Beetle; that might have been illegal even then, but no one took any notice.

Training that junior team broke the ice. Jake was the star. He was literally head-and-shoulders above the rest. I figured the only way we were going to challenge anyone was to be the best defensive team around, which meant everyone learning how to tackle.

Tackling bags were in short supply so I methodically took each boy through the correct technique. Neither Tommy nor Rowdy managed to master it – they preferred rodeo-style bulldogging.

The day came when each boy was fairly proficient, and when it did, they threw down the challenge.

'Why don't you show us how, sir?'

'I've been doing that for the last few weeks.'

'Yeah but ...'

They pointed to Jake. He grinned.

'You want me to tackle Jake?'

'Just to make sure we got it right.'

There was no way out. Jake picked up the ball and began pawing the ground like a rampaging bull. I was the helpless matador. The boys cheered and roared encouragement. To Jake, of course.

'You ready, sir?'

'Ready when you are, Jake.'

I'd played football for years but I was a show pony; I avoided tackling and had always kept my shorts clean. Now I was about to be horribly exposed, and the stakes were way higher than in any game I'd played, including grand finals.

Jake took off. He looked incredibly fearsome. I crouched and waited. He lifted his knees. I drove my shoulder into his legs and, making sure my head was to the side, made the tackle.

Thud!

Jake hit the dirt. There was silence. Jake had quite a temper. He could have leapt to his feet and decked me. But he didn't. He looked up and smiled.

'Good tackle, sir.'

The rest of the boys cheered and cat-called. Then everyone wanted a go. I tackled the whole team one at a time, including Tommy and Rowdy. Then they all tackled me. Rowdy nearly took my head off.

Rowdy and Tommy were integral parts of the team. I would let them loose for 20 minutes then drag them off before they got sent off. They treated the opposition players like they were steers at branding time. They grabbed them by their jumpers, tossed them over their hips, wrestled them to the ground and jumped on their backs. They put the fear of God into them.

We won heaps of games all over the north-west area. We travelled down the coast and flogged a few highly fancied schools down there. We were as thick as thieves and those kids became like my personal praetorian guard; whenever there was trouble on playground duty I'd whistle them up and they'd hog-tie the offenders and haul them to the deputy's office. We did everything but drink together.

The point is that I'd won them over by being forced to get to know them on their own terms. Even Rowdy and Tommy gave me a grudging respect. If I'd tried to impose my view of the world on those kids I wouldn't have gotten past first base. It was a fluke that it worked out that way, but it saved my bacon.

Staff development

While the kids might have intimidated me I approached my fellow staff members with all the confidence of youth. The fact that half of them had taught for longer than I'd been on the planet didn't phase me.

I'd already had a run-in with the librarian, Mrs Wilde. I'd sent someone to the library to get a book I needed without the proper note; that is, without following the correct procedure. To add insult to injury, I later turned up to the library with a class without having booked them in.

Never in my life have I received a shellacking to even rival the one Mrs Wilde gave me that day. She gave it to me with both barrels.

'Who do you think you are?'

'I ...'

'Do you think you own the place?'

'No ... I ...'

'What gives you the right to barge in here like Lord Muck?'

'Nothing ...'

My class, lined up behind me, were loving this.

'You'd better learn some respect, Sonny Jim.'

She shut the door in my face. Total humiliation. It didn't do much for my standing in the eyes of the kids.

Mrs Wilde had the appearance of a Viking warrior and a hair-cut that made her look like she was wearing a helmet. Everyone was scared of her and with good reason. The library was run like a well-oiled machine. No one spoke in the library.

Something told me to do my penance. I had been in the wrong: I hadn't shown Mrs Wilde the respect she deserved, nor had I bothered to learn the correct procedure. So at recess, instead of Monte Carlos I decided to devour a huge slice of humble pie. I began making the long climb upstairs to the library. I was scared shitless and expected another dressing down. The library was closed – Mrs Wilde was having her morning tea. I knocked. She put down her cuppa and made her way to the door.

'Yes?'

'Sorry to disturb you Mrs Wilde ...'

She waited.

'I just wanted to apologise for before.'

'I see.'

'I should have booked.'

'You should have.'

I was expecting another lecture when the slightest glimmer of a smile crossed her lips.

'Don't do it again.'

'I won't.'

She shut the door and returned to her cuppa.

Mrs Wilde later became my mentor and close friend. We shared many interests, including a love of politics and theatre. I spent a lot of time with her and her husband discussing the issues of the day. Their home became a kind of refuge for me. She was a warm, intelligent person with a wicked sense of humour. I often wondered what would have happened had I not apologised ...

The old saying about not judging a book by its cover certainly applied to Mrs Wilde. She was a strict disciplinarian. The smart kids loved her. No one crossed her, not even Tommy and Rowdy, although I'm not sure how much time they spent in the library. I was learning that superficial judgments were a roadblock to good teaching. The moment you put a label on someone was the moment you stopped dead in your tracks. You went nowhere. This applied to kids and to teachers.

A girl in one of my classes was a case in point. Her uniform was often filthy and she was missing a few teeth. She looked as rough as guts. Her one saving grace was a smile that could melt the hardest of hearts. Something about her made me like her. Over time we formed a close bond. She'd had a difficult upbringing but once you scratched the surface you discovered that this seemingly dysfunctional family were loving and caring and fiercely loyal to each other. Woe betide the person that bagged one of them! They were a big family and might have fallen on hard times, but they'd never stooped to self-pity. They made the most of the cards they were dealt.

Miss Eliot, my colleague on the English staff, was another case in point. She might have seemed like a character from Dickens but she was as sharp as a tack and an awesome teacher. The kids who cottoned on to her got amazing results. If I hadn't been sitting in the same staff room as Miss Eliot, I would have paid out on her. It was only because I was forced into close proximity that I got to see what a clever woman she was.

That was true of all the staff at Tenterfield High. I grew to understand that even Mr Wood had his strong suit. If you were into building things, he was the man for you. On the outside it might have seemed that he was a crazed fascist, but I soon learnt to look on the inside.

My closest friend at Tenterfield was another good example of this. He encapsulated the contradictory nature of teachers and the teaching profession. That first day when I bowled into the staff room I thought he looked familiar, but I was too busy to take much notice of him. It took us a while to warm to each other, as on the surface we didn't have much in common aside from being English/ history teachers in our first year at a high school. He'd previously been a primary teacher and was making the transition to secondary school.

His name was Les Thompson. The reason I recognised him was that I'd played football against him in Newcastle – I played for university and he for Boolaroo. The Boolaroo players used to yell things like, 'Why don't youse go home and drink your marijuana, you long-haired poofters!' In response we'd sledge them for being jailbirds, which was sort of true as a lot were on weekend release. From the safety of our cars we'd get stuck into Les for fighting on *TV Ringside*. Les was a pugilist and built like a brick shithouse; he had a good pedigree and would have been an Australian champion had he not taken up teaching in the bush.

Les was now my colleague on the English staff at Tenterfield. He was a teacher with a difference; he loved poetry and writing as much as he loved boxing and running through brick walls. The kids loved him, especially the rough-and-tumble ones. Les invited me to move in with him at Stone Age and, like me, he threw himself into the school and the town. He set up a gym at the back of The Royal. He coached and played every sport that had been invented. He was a good enough cricketer to bowl Douggie Walters in a rep game. He wasn't your standard-issue English/history teacher either. One day a boy told him to 'fuck off' in class; Les replied by picking him up by the throat and shaking the living daylights out of him. This approach wasn't exactly in the *Teacher's Manual* and you'd be sued for it now, but that boy had baited Les unmercifully for weeks, trying everything in his power to rile him. He finally succeeded. I'm not excusing Les's unconventional style; I would never have done it myself. But some kids responded to this kind of physicality. It might not have been PC but that's how it was then.

He was no fool, Les. His classes worked hard and he got great results out of them. The bright kids took the piss out of him and he gave back as good as he got. He could take a joke and he loved irony. His style as an English/history teacher bore no resemblance to Miss Eliot's more cerebral approach but he achieved similar results.

Les went on to teach in Walgett High. He lived on the banks of the Namoi River and opened his house to the Koori kids from the mission. He won the respect of whites and blacks at Walgett with his unique style of tough love. He became acting head of English and missed out on being appointed permanently to the position because he used the wrong coloured pens in his application. He could have transformed Walgett High and probably the town as well. When he missed out on the promotion he tossed it in. Another good teacher lost to the profession.

Les and I were a good team at Tenterfield. We were young and keen and determined to make a difference. Our teaching methods were poles apart but our goals were similar. We were there for the kids and we were open all hours. More than once Les came to my rescue when someone decided it was time to rearrange my features. A particular hobby of some of the young lads in the town was to turn to me in the pub, blow smoke in my face and tell me how much they hated teachers. One guy picked up my beer and poured it over my head.

'Sorry,' I replied.

It was impossible to provoke me into a fight, although nearly every young buck in town tried. I was way too much of a coward. When one particularly nasty drunk started throwing punches at me Les stepped in and the rest is history.

Joining us in our determination to change the culture of the school was a first-year-out teacher called Don, who combined teaching science with coaching cricket and soccer. Our enthusiasm at staff meetings wasn't always appreciated by our colleagues, and when I suggested a fête some of the older teachers were appalled. They had families and other commitments and organising a fête was not on their agenda. I was getting on my high horse when a voice called out:

'Why doesn't the leader of the rabble lead the bloody rabble?'

Mr Wood. That's the line I used in my play, *Us or Them*. Mrs Wilde and Miss Eliot sat through this debate bemusedly, although I think they might have enjoyed the theatre of it. Another young teacher, Jodie, had arrived on the scene. She was an art teacher and in her we had another ally. The head of maths and his wife, who was the music teacher, also swung their support behind us.

It was like a meeting of the old Labor Party, with a pro-fête faction and an anti-fête faction. There was no doubt where Mr Foster and Mr Lamb stood but the numbers were stacking up against them. I reckoned we could count on Mrs Wilde and Miss Eliot. Motions were put and argued, fists were slammed on desks. I had the distinct impression Mr Wood wished he had put a screwdriver through my eyes when he had the chance. The meeting dragged on and on. We didn't care, we had all day. We were young and single and teaching consumed our lives.

Slowly a few of the older teachers began to come around or, rather, to give up. Mr Lamb was getting impatient – he had a regular appointment to keep at the golf club. Mr Foster looked like he wished he could retire and go fishing.

The vote was called and we pulled a masterstroke by insisting on a secret ballot. The numbers were counted. We won. There was to be a fête. If looks were daggers I'd have been a dead man. It was like we'd won the federal election and I carried on like a pork chop. No wonder they thought I was a pain in the arse.

At another staff meeting the boss called for volunteers to be federation representatives. The Teachers' Federation was, and still is, one of the most powerful unions in the country. But no one wanted to be Fed Rep, it was just another hassle. Les had as much interest in politics as I had in boxing. I, on the other hand, saw it as a challenge, like coaching the footy team. I would probably have volunteered to be head cleaner if someone had asked me.

I won hands down. It was unanimous; no one else stood. I took the job very seriously. It didn't occur to me that decisions made in Sydney would not always take into account conditions in towns like Tenterfield.

At that time there were many industrial disputes around the country. To the casual observer it might have seemed that the union movement was hell bent on bringing down the Labor Party. One such dispute gripped our region and both the Tenterfield and Wallangarra meatworks were closed down for weeks. It continued over the school holidays. While the town struggled, we went away for a well-earned break on full pay, but before we did we organised an inter-school visit for the first week back. It had taken another lengthy debate to win support for the visit, but we felt these visits were vital for the kids who had little contact with other schools. The nearest was 90 kilometres away.

The day we got back from holidays I received a directive from the Teachers' Federation's regional office that we were to go on strike. It was called for the day of the inter-school visit. The strike was for a pay rise. That, coupled with the fact that the rest of the community were doing it tough because of a long-running dispute which most of them opposed, made it a very big call. I rang the regional office and pleaded our case. They were intransigent. There was to be a strike and that was that.

I however decided I couldn't go on strike and disappoint the kids. Somehow this was leaked to the *Tenterfield Star* and reported the next day:

Mr Manning, the local Teachers' Federation representative,
has called for the strike to be abandoned.

Wow! I was in the papers and apparently I also got a mention on the local ABC news. I was in the midst of a controversy and some of the older members of staff felt I was finally getting my comeuppance.

The next day in the middle of class there was a knock on the door. It was Mr Lamb.

'There's someone to see you.'

'Now?'

'Yes. I'll look after your class.'

I wondered who it could be? I walked out into the corridor and was met by a posse of very serious looking men.

'Hi.'

'Err, we're looking for Mr Manning.'

'Mr Manning? That's me.'

Their faces dropped. They looked me up and down. Here I was, all of 22 and looking about 16 with long hair, body shirt, shorts.

'You're the Fed Rep?'

'You're the one causing all the trouble?'

'Um … yeah.'

If collective hearts could sink, they did there and then. These guys had driven all the way from Tamworth to deal with the troublemaker and they were confronted with a boy. And he wasn't even in men's clothing.

We had a meeting of sorts. They pointed out the notion of union solidarity and I pointed out that I couldn't, in good conscience, go on strike. They knew I was an ingénue. They were wasting valuable time. They returned to their cars and drove back to Tamworth.

The strike went ahead and so did the inter-school visit. The staff who went donated their pay to a worthy cause. The left-wingers on staff thought I was a rat, but no one challenged for the position of Fed Rep and I retained it for the rest of the year.

When it came to decision-making, country schools and their specific conditions were not taken into account by either the department or the federation. Both were huge organisations serving the whole state; both were bureaucracies. Decisions that benefitted city schools didn't always serve the best interests of rural schools. And although the department and the federation were often at loggerheads, they were both guilty of the same short-sightedness.

Learning curve

The parallels between my life and that of the young teacher in *Wake in Fright* were eerily similar. Geographically the two towns we were sent to couldn't have been more different, but behaviourally they had much in common. The fictional town in *Wake in Fright* was called Bundanyabba or 'The Yabba' for short. Wallangarra, just across the border from Tenterfield, was known as 'The Garra'.

The Royal might not have had a two-up school quite on the same scale as the one at the pub in The Yabba but it did have some interesting characters. I recall the four brothers who came in from the mountains every blue moon. The were all in their fifties – I think they may even have fought in the war. Tough mountain men. None was married. I don't know where they lived but I did discover that the youngest wore a floral dress that matched his florid complexion. I also recall seeing a local cockie and the local tough guy going toe-to-toe in the street outside The Royal, cheered on by the mob who had spilled outside to form a human boxing ring. They fought until they were so bloodied and battered that they were both taken to hospital. I think it was a draw. It was a hell of a culture shock for a boy who might have come off a farm but who boarded at school and had a wonderfully protected time at university.

Life in a country town was a far cry from the life I'd led. In those days the further the country town was away from the Big Smoke the less it was influenced by contemporary cultural trends. There was no internet, no Facebook, no DVDs. There weren't even any videos. If you wanted the latest Cat Stevens record you had to join a record club and have it mailed out. You'd think I was talking about a hundred years ago but it's incredible how quickly life has changed in country towns today.

When I first began teaching I spent a considerable amount of my spare time at school preparing lessons and marking. I think it's a shared experience of all teachers, especially new ones. Never has 'be prepared' meant so much to so many, and for me it was a matter of survival.

While The Royal and the other four pubs were raging, Julie and Les and I sat up in the English staff room sharing resources and ideas. We tried to make our lessons vaguely relevant to the kids. For example we adapted the lyrics of contemporary musicians for our poetry lessons. Don McLean's *American Pie* was a favourite because of its slightly obscure lyrics. Kids loved Alice Cooper's *School's Out* although I'm not sure their parents were so keen on its message. Other favourites were songs like Cat Stevens' *Where Do the Children Play?* and Melanie's *Beautiful People*. We tried to connect with the kids and we didn't think that exclusively teaching Gerald Manley Hopkins and Robert Browning would work at Tenterfield in 1973. We didn't ignore the classics, we just coupled them with more contemporary lyrics.

I prepared every lesson down to the last minute. I quickly learnt that this was the only way to get through relatively unscathed, particularly with classes like 2E3 and 3E2. At that stage of my teaching career there wasn't much room for improvisation. We taught English by looking at themes and finding lots of different source material to explore them. Some themes included 'When I Have Fears', 'Out of this World', 'Con Men', 'Smoking Is a Health

Hazard', 'Speed Kills'. We found poems, songs, excerpts from plays, films, novels, short stories, anything that we could squeeze into a particular theme. These were the days when spelling and grammar took a back seat to creative expression. A typical lesson plan looked like this:

<u>People</u>

1. Creative writing *5 min*

    People are … *Class writes the ten phrases.*

2. Discuss 'people' *5 min*

    What is a person? What makes people different? What matters about people?

3. What do people have in common? *5 min*

    Write a list of all the things we share ('hope', 'fear', 'love', 'loneliness', etc.)

4. Hand out lyrics to Melanie's *Beautiful People* and Robert Frost's *An Old Man's Winter Night*

    Play song *10 min*

5. Discuss the lyrics *5 min*

    What do they mean? What is Melanie trying to say?

6. Homework *10 min*

    Make up a 'history'. What makes a person who he is? (Why is he quiet? What magazines does he read? What groups does he like? What sport does he like?)

    Your history should be a formal essay. You may include drawings and pictures and anything that adds to the portrait.

Of course, I never factored in the riots that broke out, the urgent calls of nature or the messages that came knocking at the door and needed to be read out. I was often chasing my own tail. But as far as planning was concerned I accounted for every moment, and when you consider we had 30 periods a week, that's quite a lot of preparation. And it doesn't take into account the marking, which took up many of those nights in the staff room. I wrote long, encouraging comments that were either skimmed over or not read at all. That didn't occur to me then; I had to find something positive to say about every piece of work, which is why a lot of us in those days ignored poor spelling and grammar. I wasn't going to mess up a kid's work by crossing out every second word with a red pen. I also gave a lot of 'A's. It was a habit I never kicked and it caused quite a lot of teeth-gnashing from colleagues over the years. This may have been why on my Teacher's Certificate it says:

Has a tendency to over-value the students' work.

We took our classes to heart. They weren't just another class, they were *our* classes. I don't think we saw them as a reflection of ourselves but I do know we fought tooth-and-nail for them, no matter how wild they were. It was always 'my 2E3', never just 2E3.

That's what teaching was all about in those days and I'm sure it hasn't changed in that regard. It's something that is never mentioned in the endless debates about standards and league tables and attempts at quantifying 'results'. How do you quantify that some kid was actually made to feel loved and valued? Certainly not by plastering meaningless 'scores' all over the internet.

What I learnt from that first year of teaching was that it was a much harder job than I'd ever imagined. I came to understand why some older members of staff looked like they'd had the life sucked out of them. It was tiring and demanding and, very often, confronting. The idea that teachers knocked off at 3.30 and lived the life of Riley with long undeserved holidays was absurd. A first-year-out teacher in any high school worked long hours, copped a fair bit of abuse and was tested to the end of their limits. It was tough. It sorted you out.

Every young teacher had to face moments of extreme self-doubt. Quite apart from losing control over 35-odd teenagers, there was the question of your ability to actually do any good at all. You were paranoid that a lot of the more experienced members of staff were laughing behind your back and waiting for you to fall flat on your face, which happened with monotonous regularity.

Somehow I got through that first year in one piece. At the end of it a rumour spread around the school that I was leaving. It was assumed I'd leave; if you made it through the year and you weren't settled in the town you'd either seek greener pastures or resign. Julie resigned. Les, Don and I stayed. We didn't make a pact or anything. I just think the three of us felt that if we could survive such a tough initiation, we may as well stay and reap the rewards. I did receive an offer to return to Gunnedah but I knocked it back. Maybe this got out and became general knowledge. It always amazed me how kids found out about supposedly confidential information. Staff rooms leaked like political parties.

Anyway, a bunch of 4E1 girls came up and pleaded with me to stay. This was very flattering at the time. I didn't yet realise that teenagers' allegiances can switch very rapidly and that the moment you were gone, their affections would switch to someone else and you'd be relegated to the dustbin of history. At the time I loved the attention and I loved telling the girls I'd be back. I was only 23 after all.

Gold star

The next two years' teaching at Tenterfield were some of the most satisfying of my career. In one of those wonderful quirks of fate, the replacements that came in for the departing staff members were as keen as *we* had been the year before. They threw themselves into the job. And they stayed. This continuity inevitably changed the culture of the school and had a big impact on the town.

We started a water polo club. The pool was only 33 metres long and I'd never played water polo in my life, but the pool manager suggested it and we ran with it. Soon there were eight men's and six women's teams thrashing about on a Wednesday night, watched by a few carloads of mystified locals. The teams were mainly made up of kids and teachers, plus a few local cockies and even some of the guys who'd blown smoke in my face the year before. We played together and against each other. Barriers were washed away. The maths master would be caning a boy in the afternoon and playing water polo with him at night. It was wild.

We travelled to other towns and took part in carnivals. On one occasion I took a team 299 kilometres to Tamworth to compete in a knockout competition. We were beaten in the first round. So having spent three-and-half hours getting there, we played one 20-minute game then jumped back in the car for another three-and-a-half hours. Seven hours travelling for a 20-minute game.

Admittedly we did stop over in Armidale to ensure we didn't get back to school before classes had ended. Plus the whole team – that's ten boys – were crammed into the maths master's station wagon. Try that now and see what happens!

We put on shows. I'd always dreamed of being an actor, so when the Australian Elizabethan Theatre Trust passed through town I invited them back to our new place opposite the pool, filled them with booze and relentlessly picked their brains about acting. They were living the life I fantasised about. By an odd twist of fate, when I did become an actor one of those travelling players became my agent for a while.

I put on a version of David Williamson's *The Removalists* with students playing the coppers and me as Kenny Carter. The audience of largely school kids loved seeing their teacher being bashed by kids, even if it was only on stage. Mrs Wilde came along and sat in the front row. *The Removalists* was pretty out there for those days and the language was real, which meant there were a lot of 'fucks'. I was waiting for Mrs Wilde to pull the pin but she clapped warmly at the end and commented on the veracity of the play's message. It was the first time I'd encountered a play where the characters spoke like people I knew.

At the other end of the scale – and perhaps more 'appropriately' – we did a version of *Joseph and the Amazing Technicolor Dreamcoat*. It was another staff/student collaboration and the music teacher organised the whole show. Although I entertained fantasies about becoming an actor, I knew couldn't sing to save myself. But the music teacher had a practical, if slightly deflating solution: she sang Pharaoh's part while I mimed it. God knows what the audience made of it but I had a ball! Of course, the show was a hit – in Tenterfield.

I had become very good friends with Jake and Snowy and now that I was living in more salubrious quarters opposite the pool, they kept their birds in an aviary in our yard. Another teaching mate, whom we nicknamed Pottinger after a character in the TV series *Ben Hall*, lived under the house in what could only be called rudimentary conditions. I think we paid something like five dollars a week in rent. That house became a hub of social and cultural activity as well as the site of some pretty wild parties. It was our version of the 'Yellow House'.

Our lives and the lives of the kids were intertwined in ways that would be impossible in the city. The combination of a stable and committed staff meant that the school was buzzing with activity. There was no shortage of volunteers among the staff for anything. Music flourished. School dances were regularly held. There was an art exhibition. Debating took off. Kids played in rep sporting teams. There were lots of inter-school visits and we organised a big trip to Gunnedah; a couple of bus loads of kids all decked out in school uniform – blazers, ties, the lot. This would have been inconceivable two years earlier. It was amazing.

As teachers we went to school with a spring in our step. We couldn't wait to get back from holidays. The Friday arvo procession out of town became a trickle as we hurled ourselves into local life, weekends included. We'd load up our cars and head out to Boonoo Boonoo Falls for water polo training. We took Byron on, we took Brisbane on – we took everyone on.

I'd go out fishing all night with Snowy and another kid we called Joker, and when we ran into each other in the corridor the next day it'd be:

'Morning sir.'

'Morning Snowy. Morning Joker.'

We all knew how to play the system. Did we cross boundaries? Sometimes. Were the rumours about us true? Mostly not. Did we betray trust? Never.

My last lesson in Tenterfield was held in Bruxner Park with 3E1. I'd had this class the year before when they were 2E1 and I was particularly attached to them. We'd developed an understanding that went beyond words: if someone was playing up I'd look at them and they'd stop; if I was talking crap they'd look at me in a way that made me re-think what I was saying. We trusted each other implicitly. It felt like we were a family.

This trust took time to develop, but once it was there we could do anything. They were the first class I had for drama. I'd done plays before but this was something different; this was *drama* and drama needed space, so instead of trying to conduct lessons in the classroom I came up with the bright idea of having lessons in the park.

A lot of our work was devised and we called on a range of sources. For instance, we read Judith Wright's *The Generations of Men* and created scenes from the book. We took Lewis Carroll's *Jabberwocky* and turned it into a performance piece. We used the rotunda, the willow trees, the creek; we created magic with flowers in our hair.

'Twas brillig, and the slithy toves
Did gyre and gimble in the wabe:
All mimsy were the borogoves,
And the mome raths outgrabe.

It's not surprising that some people were convinced I'd spent too much time in Nimbin. But I hadn't. Byron was more my style.

So it was appropriate that my last lesson with 3E1 was in Bruxner Park. I approached it with a certain amount of trepidation, but a very different trepidation from the one I'd felt three years earlier. I knew the kids had planned a farewell, I knew I'd have to make some sort of speech, and I knew I'd most likely lose the plot and burst into tears. I did.

I spent three years teaching in Tenterfield. I cried when I arrived and I cried when I left, and in between I made many friends and witnessed a transformation in the school which was, by and large, inspired by young, committed teachers. It was a special time. In most schools, like most workplaces, the young have to bide their time. Often all their energy has dissipated by the time they are given a chance. Or, frustrated and disillusioned by a lack of opportunity, they leave the profession altogether. We were incredibly lucky. The elders on our staff gave us the freedom to express ourselves. They were tolerant and they turned many a blind eye to our indiscretions. For whatever reason they didn't stand in the way of a bunch of young teachers who were determined to change lives.

As much as I loved it I knew it was time to move on – and it was probably best to leave before I outstayed my welcome. Besides, there were other things I still dreamt of doing, such as acting. And to do that I had to move somewhere bigger than Tenterfield.

Big School

Second period

While I left Tenterfield with a heavy heart, I was ready for change and for a return to the city, if you can call Canberra a city. My old man had moved to a small farm nearby and it gave me the chance to spend some time with him.

I had to resign from the New South Wales Department of Education if I wanted to teach in Canberra: different state, different system. It was a bit like getting a train to Brisbane from Sydney – you had to change trains at Wallangarra because the railway gauges in New South Wales and Queensland were different sizes. Every state in Australia had its own school system and its own railway line. We really didn't get it right at Federation.

I went in search of a teaching job. My first port of call was a place called the School Without Walls, a progressive school loosely based on Summerhill. On the surface it seemed that I'd be well suited to a 'free-spirited' environment. I had long hair, I surfed, I drove a Kombi and I loved Melanie, but contrary to popular belief I was never a hippy – nor had I ever smoked a joint with one of my students! The truth was, I was relatively straight.

So when I rolled up at the School Without Walls for an interview and saw kids lolling about smoking, I was horrified. I was informed that the kids ran the show: they turned up to class when they felt like it; if they were bored, they wandered outside and lit up a gasper; if they didn't like what you were teaching, they told you – and you were expected to change it. Great.

After the rigours of teaching at Tenterfield I wasn't ready for this kind of anarchy. I pictured myself spending hours preparing a lesson only to have half the class wander out in the middle of it. I didn't mind the concept of empowering kids, as long as it was done within boundaries. For a supposed hippy-trippy type I was very much a believer in boundaries. I still am. The School Without Walls and I parted company.

I scored a job at Watson High School on Canberra's north side. Watson was a working-class suburb with a high percentage of migrant families. The school had a reputation for being pretty rough-and-tumble, with a lot of kids from broken homes. It was a big school too with nearly a thousand kids, one-third the size of the whole of Tenterfield!

I arrived in Canberra at a time when the entire school system there was being revolutionised. Kids in Years 11 and 12 were able to go to colleges and Watson's Year 12 in 1976 were the last ones in the old system. They were caught in a time warp, with their friends at college being given freedoms in Year 11 that they were still denied in Year 12. But most of them just laughed it off, choosing instead to take neither school nor their teachers very seriously. These kids were also more street-smart than the kids at Tenterfield. They were young adults; some of the boys had beards. They rode motorbikes and were legally able to drink in pubs. The girls looked like they were in their twenties, hip and cool and ready for life. A 17-year-old shouldn't be expected to behave like a pre-pubescent 12-year-old. It only creates a lot of unnecessary conflict. The more you try to stop kids growing up the more trouble you are likely to have.

The college system made sense. Students weren't forced to wear uniforms, they could go home when their classes were over, they called the teachers by their first names, and they could smoke, always a symbol of maturity and approaching adulthood. They may not have had as much latitude as the students at the School Without Walls, but they were encouraged to be responsible for their own decisions and this seemed to set them up well for tertiary studies.

It has always fascinated me that kids from rigid school environments often struggle with the freedom of university. Many private-school kids bomb out in their first year because they've never had to organise themselves, or even think for themselves. They've always been told what to do. I went to one of the most rigid private schools on earth, but as I was totally disengaged from it in my last few years and never did as I was told, the freedom of university suited me down to the ground. I think most kids benefit from taking responsibility for their own actions and are well and truly over being spoon fed by the time they reach Years 11 and 12.

At Watson there was a clash between the demands of the old and new systems. Many teachers didn't like the idea of giving 17- and 18-year-olds so much freedom. They preferred the status quo. In fact, they probably preferred the status over the quo. They were afraid of relinquishing any power – and the respect they thought this power deserved. I often wondered if these teachers got the respect they thought they deserved at home. I doubt it. More than a few felt threatened by individuality and difference. They believed in conformity and order: the timetable and the bell.

Do some people become teachers because they love rules? I don't know, but I do know that some teachers love power. They love shouting at kids and asserting their authority. The truth of the matter is that about halfway through Year 8 most kids stop taking any notice of teachers who rant and rave. They learn to suffer in silence and the tantrums have little effect on them. They wait till the storm has passed and then get on with whatever they were doing.

I can vouch from personal experience that caning is like that. The more I got belted as a kid the less effect it had. In fact, I wore my record for most beltings in a year as a badge of courage. There was plenty of caning, to absolutely no effect, at Tenterfield. I never caned anyone and always favoured the carrot over the stick. It's incredible to think that caning was not abolished in New South Wales state schools until 1987. Victoria led the way by banning it in 1983; in Queensland it was banned in 1992. Of course, if you want your kids to get a good flogging you can always send them to a private school!

The boss at Watson High was an interesting chap. His name was Mr McDougall. Even when I'd been teaching there for two years I still called him Mr McDougall. He never really warmed to me. He definitely thought I was a hippy-trippy type but, then again, he was a 1950s kind of guy. The whole '60s revolution had passed him by. He probably thought I'd benefit from a good caning.

The fact that a lot of the staff reflected old values created inevitable tension between staff and students and within the staff itself. Interestingly this divide wasn't always generational and almost never determined by gender. It was about attitude and open-mindedness. It may also have had something to do with self-esteem; some teachers may have hidden behind a security blanket of archaic rules to protect them from their own insecurities. This was more evident at Watson than at Tenterfield. Without realising it, Tenterfield had been more progressive, maybe because it was so small and so far away.

Staff meetings at Watson, like in nearly every school on the planet, were interminable. They went on and on and on. We discussed such weighty issues as what colour pen to use when writing reports and the ubiquitous question of smoking in the toilets. We were treated like pre-schoolers; we were regularly reminded of our responsibilities and given 'a good talking to'. Like assemblies, staff meetings followed a familiar pattern and, like assemblies, almost no one paid any attention to the lectures on picking up rubbish on playground duty and getting to class on time. Staff meetings were an opportunity for the 'executive' to reaffirm the hierarchical nature of the school and for the rest of us to do crosswords, catch up on marking, dream of greener pastures or stare wistfully at our watches. It might be okay to remind kids of their place but it doesn't do much for someone in their fifties who has been teaching for 30 years.

Staff meetings involved serious role playing. The executive took charge out the front and the rest of the staff occupied the bleachers. Meetings were often conducted in a classroom, which only served to reinforce the feeling among the staff that they were barely out of nappies. A perfectly reasonable person who happened to be a deputy would role-play the sergeant major when addressing their colleagues. They would call good friends 'Mr' or 'Miss':

'Would Mr X and Miss Y make sure they remember to wipe their bottoms.'

If there is one thing that gets up teachers' noses, it is that they are almost never treated as the professionals they clearly are. At every turn they are undermined and undervalued. The system promotes this. As everyone knows, teachers come in all shapes and sizes. Why do we persist with this absurd 'one size fits all' approach? If kids at colleges in Canberra were allowed to go home when their classes were over, why weren't teachers afforded the same privileges? Why should someone who doesn't have classes after lunch be forced to hang around till the bell rings at 3.30? Couldn't we trust a responsible adult to act responsibly? Staff rooms are not conducive to work – they are noisy, volatile places. Why not encourage teachers to go home and do their marking and prepare their lessons in a comfortable environment? They might even get some work done.

Staff meetings took place with monotonous regularity. Even if there was nothing to report, there'd still be a staff meeting. Every Thursday, come hell or high water, we'd troop into the designated classroom and dutifully take our places.

'It has come to my attention ...'

And away they'd go. Staff meetings give that keen-as-mustard bore the chance to rabbit on about the bleeding obvious. It was always the same few who felt the pressing need to raise a query or point of order just as the rest of us were reaching for our keys. We'd sink back into our seats and exhale loudly. And no sooner would they finish airing their concerns than the bright-as-a-button, ambitious young thing would leap to his feet to remind everyone that he was 'executive material'. Maybe I was like this when I first started teaching at Tenterfield and was now getting my just desserts. It's possible, but it wasn't long before I grew out of it.

Unlike the Tenterfield elders, the mob of troglodytes who ran the show at Watson weren't going to roll over easily on anything. They insisted on protocols, and the more they insisted the more we tried to break them. It was a bit like open warfare. Mind you, open warfare is common in staff rooms.

Half the staff at Watson dressed in suits and ties or, when they were letting their hair down, shorts and long socks. Their female counterparts dressed like they were members of the Country Women's Association. A few dressed to remind everyone that teaching was really beneath them, that they were really very rich and their husbands incredibly important. Some gave new meaning to the phrase 'mutton dressed as lamb'.

In the other camp were those who looked like they'd just got out of bed – which in some cases was probably true – or were on the way home from Woodstock. One or two dressed way too provocatively, which may have been the point. Jeans and colourful shirts were common. The physical education staff wore shorts and

T-shirts and rode to work on bikes. They were pretty cool.

Even though I was officially an English/history teacher I had a couple of periods of PE. This, coupled with the fact that I now saw myself as a drama teacher, meant I inclined towards the PE uniform of shorts and T-shirt.

In fact, my evolution as a teacher was reflected in my garb. When I started teaching I thought I'd better dress like an adult, so I bought lots of 'grown-up' clothes. As I started to work out what teaching was really about, I reassessed my dress code. The tie was loosened and discarded. The groovy body shirts and matching permanent press 'slacks' were flicked along with the shorts and long socks. They were replaced with jeans, T-shirts, flannos, sweat-shirts and, in Canberra, duffle coats and beanies.

This had nothing to do with fashion statements, it was about the nature of the work. More often than not you were in a hurry; you'd be out on the oval coaching kids and have a class next period, so you didn't have time for a shower and a change of clothes. If the choice was looking neat and tidy or getting stuck in, I'd get stuck in every time.

Over the years I noticed kids becoming more self-conscious about their body odour. I don't recall anyone at Tenterfield reaching for the Lynx; nowadays they only have to walk around the room once before they're spraying it all over themselves. When I complained that the classroom smelt like a teenager's bedroom, they'd ignore me; when I told them their natural body odour was preferable to the stink of the crap they were spraying everywhere, they'd look at me like I'd lost my marbles. I would have passed out if we hadn't had windows. God knows what happens in all those private schools with air conditioning.

Naturally Mr McDougall didn't approve of the way I dressed. In fact he seemed far more concerned with how I looked than my actual teaching. I tried to point out that drama was a practical subject, like PE, but he didn't buy it. He didn't buy me. About once a week there'd be a little note in my pigeon hole when I got to school, initialled with his first name:

See me. A.

So at the end of the day I'd make my way to the principal's office. There'd be a row of naughty kids lined up to get their dose of punishment. I'd take my place at the end of the queue and when it was my turn to take the medicine, he'd call me in.

'Next!'

The first thing I'd do before Mr McDougall could open his mouth was to apologise.

'I'm sorry, Mr McDougall.'

He'd always look surprised, as if he'd expected me to defend myself.

'Mmm?'

'It won't happen again.'

We never got to defining the 'it'. My admission of guilt always stumped him. He would look me up and down suspiciously. I wasn't exactly a picture of sartorial elegance: hair all over the place, T-shirt and shorts on the grubby side, socks around my ankles, runners the worse for wear. I was his worst nightmare.

'Yes, well …'

He'd wave his hand around, searching for words.

'Just had PE. Sorry.'

Now this wasn't strictly true; I only had one double period of PE in a load of 35 periods and Mr McDougall knew this. But I did have drama and I did run around the oval with the kids at recess and lunchtime. He'd just shuffle his papers.

'I've had some complaints about the noise …'

'Yeah, sorry about that. We're doing the Witches' scene at the moment. The *Scottish* play?'

Nudge nudge, wink wink. But instead of getting the joke or

even the reference, he'd probably be fantasising about pulling out a dagger and stabbing me in the throat.

'Won't happen again. Promise.'

It was a wonderful stalemate. We both knew I didn't mean it, but what could he do? Sack me? The only way you could get sacked was if you were caught red-handed having sex with a student in the playground or shooting up in front of a class. And even then the federation would probably defend you. I knew of a teacher who sold dope to kids and got away with it.

From time to time Mr McDougall would appear at the door of my classroom and peer through the window. He wasn't a big man; he was a bit like Inspector Clouseau, although I never saw him hiding behind a pot plant! The kids would gesture towards the door and I'd look around and see his head duck down. He might have been taking notes. But even if he'd been taking photos on his iPhone, as might happen today, he wouldn't have seen much: kids lying on the floor breathing into the pits of their stomachs or walking in diagonals across the room; we walked through mud, climbed stairs, imagined we were butterflies. It was all pretty innocent. There was certainly nothing radical about it. I was doing acting classes outside school hours at the Canberra Rep and I used to try out the things we did on the kids. They loved it. Even the more self-conscious kids got into drama as long as you didn't single them out to deliver a long-winded Shakespearean monologue, which I never did.

If I caught Mr McDougall spying on us I'd invite him in. I'm not sure what he made of a room full of kids rolling around on the floor being 'earthworms' but he never said anything or asked any questions, so we'd just carry on as though he wasn't there. It was an odd relationship I had with Mr McDougall. He never really challenged me even when he would have been perfectly within his rights to do so.

I decided we needed a drama room, even though drama wasn't a stand-alone subject in those days, so I encouraged the kids to be creative and decorate the classroom in which I held most of my lessons. I didn't bother to get anyone's permission. I just lobbed down to the art room and grabbed some paint and brushes from a mate on the staff. The first thing we did was to paint the door white and to emblazon it with the Rolling Stones' emblematic 'tongue and lips' logo from the inside sleeve of their *Sticky Fingers* album. Mr McDougall could have charged me with vandalising school property but he never mentioned it; nor did he comment on the 'stoned crow' the kids had painted above my desk. Perhaps he was just waiting for me to go away.

It was around this time that I started questioning whether I was cut out for teaching. I was getting sick of being hauled before principals and having to keep an eye out for them. The idea of seeking a principal's approval seemed like something a child would do; and I'd been doing it one way or another for as long as I could remember. Deep down, I was getting sick of having to justify myself to a 'boss'.

Class act

Like all schools, Watson had a lot of great teachers. There was a woman called Monica Fulbright on the English staff who was bit like Miss Eliot at Tenterfield. She insisted on being called Monica. She was a dynamo. She was well into her forties or even her fifties, but we never discussed her age, she was too busy inspiring kids for small talk. She didn't take any nonsense from anyone and the kids loved her. She was scathing about the conservative faction on the staff. She loved English and her love for the subject was transfused into her charges.

Monica reminded me of my stepmother, Barbara, who was also a remarkable teacher. Think of Maggie Smith at her most regal and you're on the right track. By a strange twist of fate Barbara began teaching in a small country school the same year I was sent to Tenterfield. Before that she'd been teaching at Cheltenham Girls High on Sydney's North Shore. Her kids at Cheltenham regularly topped the state in ancient history, which was her particular specialty. Barbara married my father in her fifties, an interesting career move, and moved into our farm at Rylstone. This meant she had to leave her 'gels' at Cheltenham. She took a job teaching at Kandos High. Kandos was the poor relation to Rylstone; Rylstone was a 'cockies' town while Kandos was a working-class 'cement' town. Where Tenterfield had the meatworks, Kandos had the cement works and the whole town was covered in cement dust. It was a bit like one of those Welsh mining towns in *How Green Was My Valley*.

Barbara and I used to discuss teaching and tactics. We shared a love of ancient history, English literature and theatre. Even though we were nearly 40 years apart, we were both learning the ropes as far as teaching in a small country town was concerned. If Kandos was a bit of a culture shock for Barbara, she was a revelation for Kandos. The kids had never encountered 'cultivated English' or for that matter a teacher who was a member of the Queen's Club in Sydney. We both agreed that the key to survival was to throw ourselves into school life whatever the cost. I remember waking up in the middle of the night back at the farm to see the light on in Barbara's bedroom; she was burning the midnight oil, marking essays and preparing lessons. It was the way of the dedicated teacher.

Barbara might have appeared as out of her depth at Kandos as I was at Tenterfield, but she emphatically rose to the challenge. She produced plays. She introduced the kids to Noel Coward – God knows what they or their parents made of him. She staged a grand production of a Molière play that involved parents sewing costumes and making wigs. She even roped in my old man to build sets.

When a boy decided to take her on at Kandos she was ready for it.

'Fuck off,' he told her.

'Dear boy, I can say "fuck" as easily as you can. Please try to broaden your vocabulary.'

He nearly fell off his chair. Needless to say by the end of the year she had them eating out of her hand and the rough nut who'd told her to fuck off took his place in the chorus decked out in wig and tights.

Dynamic teachers change lives and more often than not they speak the same language as their students. The art and PE staff at

Watson were like that; what's more, they'd organise exhibitions and sporting events galore, which enabled teachers to meet the kids on neutral territory, outside the confines of the classroom. This facilitated the breaking down of barriers.

I've never been able to work out why compulsory competitive sport between schools was ditched in some states. We bang on about health and fitness but we don't offer practical opportunities to our kids. Apart from the obvious benefits of general fitness and better staff–student relationships, competitive sport offers kids who mightn't set the world on fire academically the chance to shine. Kids love pulling on the school jumper, no matter how daggy it is. They identify with their school. Kids of all ages and abilities used to play sports against each other on Wednesday afternoons; the results of the games were immaterial and almost immediately forgotten. Replacing team sports with 'recreational activities' was a decision by the department and Teachers' Federation that just didn't make sense.

This goes for more than just sport; extra-curricular activities of all persuasions open doors that might otherwise remain closed to kids. Why not make them easier to access, not harder? Why regard them with suspicion, as if the teachers spending all that time on them were up to no good? Strangely it was often the teacher who wouldn't work in an iron lung who complained the loudest when other teachers went beyond the call of duty for the kids.

When I arrived at Watson there was still a Rugby Union competition between schools. It was a knockout comp open to public and private schools. Somehow I got the coaching gig. We had a few more players to draw on than we did at Tenterfield; I had a full team of senior, seasoned footballers, some of whom were pretty tough nuts. We won our way through the early rounds and came up against Daramalan College in the semi-finals. Daramalan was a private Catholic school that was known as a football nursery; it had a fearsome reputation and produced many Australian players. Being a state school, most of our kids were League players. Private schools played Rugby Union. We didn't care. We'd give 'em a run for their money even though we were at very long odds and they were the unbackable favourites.

The semi-final was a home game for us, which meant we got to choose when and where it would be played. Without asking anyone I programmed kick-off for the beginning of lunch. This would maximise support for our team. We ran out just as the bell was ringing. It was fantastic! The whole school descended on the oval and lined up along the sidelines. It was like a scene from *Tom Brown's Schooldays*. Our boys grew ten-feet tall when they saw the crowd and heard the chant: 'Watson! Watson! Watson!' It's amazing how boys will lift when there are a few hundred girls cheering them on. 'Darra' was an all-boys school and our girls gave them heaps. The Darra kids didn't know what hit them.

Unfortunately I hadn't factored in that the game ran for 70 minutes and lunch was only 40. This meant the whole school would be late for class – and it would be my fault. Bells rang. Mr McDougall and the deputies ran up and down the sidelines trying to get the kids back into class. No one was going to move. Eventually they gave up and joined in the cheering.

Spurred on by these amazing scenes the boys played out of their skins and we won the game. It was the biggest upset in years. The place erupted. It took forever to get the rest of the school back to class. I'm not sure much learning took place that afternoon but it was a mighty victory and it united the school.

There was also a fair crowd for the 'staff versus students' game. It was a grudge match with a difference. It was played in a good spirit: no biffo but plenty of hard tackling. That's right, tackling. Serious body contact. Occupational health and safety wasn't on the agenda that afternoon. It was a sign of the times that we could play

Year 12 in a game of footy. There might have been a few bruised egos but no one was seriously hurt. Well, that's not entirely true. When we had a 'staff versus students' game at Tenterfield I was collected by a covering tackle and broke four ribs. I think the boy who tackled me was sending me a message. There was no real harm done though. We all shook hands and most likely treated each other with a little more respect thereafter.

Drama began to consume my life in and out of school. I acted in a few plays at Canberra Rep with a real director who worked in professional theatre. It was a fair way from *Doctor in the House* at the Tenterfield School of Arts. I even got a couple of good reviews and my fantasies of an acting career started looking a little less far-fetched.

At school we started putting on shows at lunchtime and at night. We did some self-devised stuff that was considered a bit 'out there' because of all the drug references. I didn't see the point in pretending the kids weren't into drugs; quite a few of them would turn up to class off their faces. This never happened at Tenterfield. Instead of ignoring it I asked them whether they'd consider drinking a six-pack before school. After a while most of them gave up smoking dope at lunchtime – they had too much to do. We did a musical without a single member of staff backstage. The kids put the whole thing together themselves: set, costumes, props, sound, even ticket collection. It's incredible what motivated kids can achieve.

Putting shows on is a big deal in schools, whether they be primary or high schools. Teachers and kids share a common goal and the rules of engagement are totally different from what both groups are used to in the classroom. There is always plenty of drama both on and off the stage, but no matter what the final performance is really like, everyone is empowered by the experience.

The Year 10 group that staged the musical had a terrible reputation among the staff. They were a feisty bunch. They pushed boundaries but, when you got into their heads, they were capable of great things. I probably had more in common with them than I did with a lot of my colleagues. This was more an indication of my own immaturity than a comment on the rest of the staff – I had yet to learn the importance of the 'separation of teachers and students'. I was too young and too wrapt up in my own Messiah complex to take any notice of anyone else.

A case in point was the farewell assembly for this notorious Year 10 group. It was originally going to be a big event with the whole school gathered to give them an appropriate send off. But the kids had trashed the school and, quite rightly, Mr McDougall had cancelled the celebrations. The kids were pissed off; they trudged into the hall where only a handful of teachers had gathered to wave them off. Mr McDougall gave it to them with both barrels, telling them in no uncertain terms that he was glad to be rid of them. When I was called up to receive a present, I made a point of saying how I thought they were the most amazing kids I'd ever taught. It was a bit over the top.

My two worlds collided at the end of that year when I wrote, produced and acted in a play about teaching called *Us or Them*. I'd never written a play before and had absolutely no idea what I was doing. I wrote it in a fit of pique after I'd missed out on the role of the boy in *Equus*.

Us or Them signalled the end of the first incarnation of my teaching career. We staged it at Childers Street Hall and even though it was deeply flawed, it was surprisingly successful. It was directed by a member of the English staff, a guy whom I never thought had any interest in theatre. That's how self-absorbed I was.

The cast consisted of some regulars in the Canberra theatre scene, a couple of mates, some members of staff and some kids from Year 10. I played the rather self-righteous young radical who thought he knew it all.

It might have been slightly autobiographical.

Bran Nue World

After recess

As they say, it's funny how things happen.

Us or Them attracted quite a bit of attention, including a story in *The Australian*. This led to my heading up to Sydney to test the acting waters. I turned up at Shanahan's, the leading actors' agent at the time, and presented my credentials, which were non-existent. I didn't even have a biography let alone a '10x8', which is a publicity shot of yourself looking as appealing as possible. Like Manuel in *Fawlty Towers*, 'I knew nothing.'

And I got nothing. I returned to Canberra and began an acting career in the local professional theatre. I played Ahmed in Alex Buzo's *Norm and Ahmed*. The production coincided with The National Playwrights' Conference in Canberra and – guess what? – I was invited to join Shanahan's. So began a life of acting and writing.

Talk about landing on your feet. I arrived in Sydney at the height of the 10BA, the notorious tax-incentive scam that enabled heaps of dodgy films to be made along with some great ones. Film and television production was booming, so even a novice like me got work. In fact, I got heaps of work; it was mind-blowing how lucky I was. I even realised a couple of boyhood fantasies: I got to play cricket for Australia (*Bodyline*) and to star in a movie (*Dead End Drive-In*). *Us or Them* got picked up by the Griffin Theatre Company and was a surprising hit, playing extended seasons and being performed all over the place. But despite being busy I became restless during the inevitable downtimes an actor experiences; even though I was writing lots of plays, something was missing.

In 1989 I saw an ad in the local paper calling for teachers at the Eora Centre for Aboriginal Visual and Performing Arts in Redfern. It was the year after the Bicentenary and, like a lot of whitefellas, I felt it was time to get off my arse and do something for Indigenous Australians. I hadn't taught since Watson but I thought I might still be able to contribute something.

I went in and met Bobby Merritt. Bobby had written the ground breaking play *The Cake Man*. He had established Eora without any funding support and was determined to create an acting school for Indigenous performers. I told him I had some spare time on my hands and would like to offer my services. I added that I didn't expect to be paid. He told me to come in the next day.

Eora was situated in the old CES building in Regent Street, Redfern. The building was a cement edifice of the type favoured by the Soviets and adopted by Australian government bureaucracies in the 1970s. You walked off the street and into a foyer that doubled as a 'learning space'. There was an office and a make-shift stage; in the corner an area had been partitioned off to serve as a staff room. The rest was open space. Upstairs was the visual arts department and downstairs were some rudimentary classrooms and a car park. Next door was the CES office. Quite often someone would stumble into one of my drama classes looking for their dole cheque.

If the physical environment was cold and uninviting, the vibe of the place was quite the opposite. There was a tangible sense of possibility. Bobby Merritt wasn't interested in being told how to do things by whitefellas. He saw blackfellas creating their own narratives, telling their own stories, doing it themselves. He was a visionary.

I went in the next day and saw a mob of blackfellas congregating in the foyer. I stood around feeling like a fish out of water – there weren't a lot of whitefellas there. It turned out to be a kind of orientation or meeting day. Everyone was chatting and it was all very informal. Bob Maza got up and made a bit of a speech. Like Bobby Merritt, Bob Maza was a legend. He'd been at the forefront of the Black Theatre movement and was a movie star to boot, having just starred in Bruce Beresford's *The Fringe Dwellers*. Bob welcomed everyone and sort of outlined what was going to happen during the year. Then he returned to the job at hand.

'Seeing as we're celebrating being invaded, I thought we might have a bit of a debate. Ned here, he's a new teacher, he can argue Captain Cook's side of the argument and I'll put ours.'

And he sat down, grinning.

I didn't know what to do or where to look. After a while he wandered over, put his arm around me and smiled.

'You'll be okay.'

Then he left me to it.

What was I going to do? Stand up in front of a crowd of blackfellas and argue what a good idea it was to take their country from them? This was 1989, a year since the big celebrations and an emotionally charged time. I decided it was a case of no-guts-no-glory. I was an actor, I could play a baddie – although until then I'd rarely been cast as one. There was one slight problem. Would these guys know I was debating? Would they know I didn't believe all the stuff I was sprouting? Was I nervous? I was shitting myself.

Bob got to his feet. He was a loved and revered elder, whereas I was a blow-in from Balmain. The only thing I had going for me was the presence of some Tigers fans in the audience.

The debate got underway. Bob argued the blackfellas' case forcefully and passionately. I wondered if he was testing my mettle. The more the crowd cheered the more nervous I became. When he finished there was clapping and cheering.

'Now we'll hear the whitefellas' side of the story.'

I got up and looked out at my audience. They weren't exactly welcoming. I began to wonder if I'd get out of there in one piece. I took a deep breath.

'1788 marked a turning point in the history of this land. The arrival of the First Fleet heralded the civilizing of the continent.'

You can imagine how this went down. I ploughed on.

'Until the arrival of the First Fleet this country was empty. *Terra nullius* was the term Cook used when he discovered it, this ... *empty land*.'

Murmurs, challenging looks.

I carried on regardless, arguing how civilisation came to the Great South Land and how the British settlement was the best thing since sliced bread. The interjections became louder and more threatening.

'Come on, give him a go.'

I could see Bob Maza was enjoying this. Out of the corner of my eye I saw Bobby Merritt leaning against the wall. He was enjoying it too. Talk about a baptism of fire.

Strangely, Bob won the debate. I didn't get a single vote when the decision was made with a show of hands. Bob called for quiet.

'Give young Ned here a hand. He's been a good sport.'

There was desultory applause. He put his arm around me again.

'That was good. Well done – they liked you.'

The Koori sense of humour. The truth is they were too busy cheering him to take much notice of me. I was learning about being superfluous.

Teaching at Eora was unlike anything I'd encountered before. For a start, it was a tertiary institution, although 'institution' is hardly the right word. At that stage it was independently run; it would later be taken over by TAFE, who run it to this day. I had no idea where its funding came from or how it functioned. All I knew was that it was Bobby Merritt's brainchild. I didn't ask a lot of questions. I'd stumbled into a hotbed of creative energy at a time when not many whitefellas knew about its existence. Blackfellas knew about it; they knew about everything to do with blackfellas. The Koori grapevine. Even though I was married to an Indigenous woman and had come into contact with the community, I had never been involved in this kind of way. The scales were about to be removed from my eyes.

Performing arts covered drama, creative writing, piano, guitar and composition. I was to take drama and creative writing. Bobby Merritt told me to insist on 'industry standards' and to demand things like attendance and punctuality. I was to ignore 'Koori time', although I was yet to fully understand the term. I was to set high standards and insist upon them.

Easier said than done.

What struck me most when I first walked into Eora was a sense of incredible pride and ownership. Everyone in that foyer was celebrating. Celebrating that they're made it this far. Now they were going to kick some serious goals. They weren't interested in second best; they wanted their work to come under the same critical microscope that was applied to whitefellas' work.

The student body was like nothing I had ever come across. There were men and women of *all* ages, people who had lived lives most of us couldn't imagine in our wildest dreams. There were mothers who had raised families and others in the process of doing so. There were youngsters with stars in their eyes. There were those who had done and seen it all, some of it on the wrong side of the law. Quite a few were battling with demons and a couple who hoped Eora would offer a way out of the mire of various addictions. Some were completely re-imagining themselves; they were starting a brand new chapter and they saw Eora as a pathway to gaining the practical skills they needed, like the confidence to speak in public or, more basically, to read and write. There were people who could draw and paint and sing and play music but who needed to hone and develop these skills. A few dreamt of becoming actors or professional musos or even pop stars. I don't think any of the visual artists dreamt of fame and fortune, but some achieved it anyway. Then there were those who wanted to write; they weren't sure whether it would be a play or a film or a novel, but they knew they wanted to write. And they all had a story to tell.

Some had no clear reason to be at Eora. They weren't necessarily after anything; they just wanted to be there, to see what was happening, to be somewhere safe. Eora was special because it was an *Aboriginal* performing and visual arts centre. It was theirs at a time when not much else was. This is Bobby Merritt's great legacy. He might have dreamt of a blackfellas' NIDA but it became far more important than that. It was somewhere to find a brother, a sister, a 'coz', an uncle or an auntie. It was somewhere that would understand *them*.

Eora was at the centre of a revolution of sorts. In 1988 there was a sense that Indigenous Australia had reached a crossroads. While many white Australians celebrated the Bicentenary by joyously re-enacting the arrival of the First Fleet, Indigenous Australians mourned the invasion of their land. The Survival Day March brought people to Sydney from all over the country. And if there was one dominant emotion during the march and at the concerts and gatherings, it was pride – for having survived the abuses of the past 200 years – and this pride translated into a determination to celebrate all that was good about being an Indigenous Australian. They were going to be positive about the future and to make it work for them.

For those who dreamt of greatness, Eora was the place to be. You could sense there was something special going on. The art room was a case in point. There wasn't much light or fresh air in there but the place was alive with ideas. It was like someone had opened the floodgates and rivers of bottled-up imagination had been released. The work was extraordinary in its originality and depth. It didn't matter that the conditions were hardly conducive to making anything, let alone art – once the opportunity presented itself, nothing was going to stop this mob. Some truly great artists and perhaps even a whole art movement came out of the art room. Talk about finding your voice.

Music was always pumping out of the art room. In fact, it was always pumping out of Eora. All types of music, live and recorded. One day I could hear an impromptu concert getting underway. I remember thinking, God, that guy sounds like Jimmy Little. I climbed on a chair to check him out and it *was* him. Jimmy Little! His song 'Royal Telephone' had relegated the Beatles to second place on the hit parade. I nearly fell off the chair. I was introduced to one of this country's greats and we were to become lifelong friends. We did a show together called *Black Cockatoos* at the Belvoir St Theatre. I directed Jimmy, after a fashion, while he taught me all about humility and professionalism.

Some of the people leading the way at Eora had already achieved greatness, like Jimmy Little and Bob Maza, but they went about their business in the most unobtrusive way. They never felt the need to announce themselves. Their message was that anyone can do it.

'Hey bud, it's no big deal. You can do this. We're all in it together.'

For someone who had been working in theatre, film and television for 12 years, this was quite a revelation; let alone for someone who had spent a lifetime in a school system that is obsessed with hierarchy. Not to say that there wasn't any tension at Eora; tension was inevitable, particularly in a teaching environment where the very role of the teacher, the authority figure, could be seen to represent everything that had damaged the Aboriginal people.

If I didn't have much in the way of status at Tenterfield or Watson, I had even less at Eora. For the first time in my life I experienced what it was like to be in the minority. I was the odd one out in every situation. I was armed with a little knowledge and that was it. Some people there were suspicious of my motives. On more than one occasion I'd catch someone looking at me as if to say, 'What are you doing here, bud? What do you want?'

For a lot of Indigenous Australians it was a time of connecting or re-connecting, of having the confidence to identify themselves as black. This meant coming to terms with their heritage, which, in many cases, meant acknowledging their Aboriginality for the first time. It was big stuff. It was life and death. It was something I was yet to fully comprehend.

It was also a time for soul-searching among a lot of white Australians. We were aware of the terrible harm inflicted upon Indigenous Australia and we wanted to find ways to redress the balance. Most of the teachers were there, like me, to contribute to what we felt was a worthy cause. Very genuine. Some might say very patronising. Of course the blackfellas at Eora saw us coming and they played us like a fiddle, provoking all sorts of weird and conflicting behaviour from some of the white teachers.

A couple of the women on staff were serious feminists. They would take a 'no shit from no one' approach to matters of sexual equality – unless it happened to be from black students. One Koori guy delighted in pushing these boundaries. Feminist ideology wasn't a high priority for many blackfellas at Eora and sexism sometimes raised its ugly head. This particular dude flirted unashamedly with the female teachers. He said and did things that made me squirm, but because of his Aboriginality he got away with it.

Double standards? That's what can make working in culturally diverse places tricky. Social changes that we take for granted aren't necessarily adopted by every community. What's good for middle-class white folk may not be a priority for cultures with different agendas, such as surviving.

The racist card was never far from being pulled out. Us white-fellas were easy targets and were super-sensitive about it – the last thing we wanted to be called was a racist. The blackfellas at Eora knew that and some played that card when it suited them. Some-times they were taking the piss, sometimes they were using it to justify their own unacceptable behaviour, sometimes they were on the money. It was complicated.

There was an incident when a maths teacher was king hit. It was a cowardly act and there was some confusion over the best way to deal with it. It brought the issue of being a white teacher in a black world into sharp focus. Would we pretend it didn't happen or would we throw the book at the assailant? In the end the assail-ant left. I'll never know if he did this of his own volition.

Teaching at Eora forced me to re-examine lots of things, not least my understanding of the 'Koori way'. What did that phrase mean? Did it excuse any kind of behaviour? Could men be disrespectful to women and find some justification for it? And what about time? It may have had a different meaning in traditional culture but when you were conducting a class, time was of the essence. It didn't work if people came and went as they pleased. It didn't work at the School Without Walls and it didn't work here. At the very start I was told to insist on punctuality. If I had a quid for the number of times I heard one Koori say to another 'Don't give me that Koori time shit' I'd be a rich man. Most Kooris at Eora had no truck with that – they wanted to get stuff done and so did I. How do you put a show on in Koori time? How do you put it on in any time if half the cast isn't there? The only way I was going to survive was to play the ball not the person. I applied the same standards that I applied wherever I taught. It was all about getting the work done. And it worked.

In my first year a couple of my students did play on the notion of Koori time and the fact that I was a whitefella. They didn't stay the distance.

What really blew me away was how people genuinely supported each other and also the notion of 'respect'. All the youngies showed respect for their elders. It was demanded of them. So was respect for traditions and culture. 'Respect' was a word that began to take on a new meaning for me; it was a long way from the respect some teachers demand.

This issue of respect also had its humorous side. Some of the 'oldies' thought the youngsters weren't showing respect for themselves in the way they dressed. In that at least, the generational divide is always the same, no matter what the culture.

I had to be constantly on my toes and whenever something blew up between students, I butted out. I wasn't privy to the history between them so it was best to make myself invisible, particularly if it got physical. Even in a school situation it's often wise not to intervene in a fight. I stepped in between a boy and a girl who were going at it hammer-and-tongs at Tenterfield and they both turned on me. The girl in question attacked me with a chair!

I was witness to a few ugly incidents in the early days at Eora. I was conducting a class in the foyer when this guy burst in. He was one of the most striking men I had ever seen. He was tall and muscular and, I later discovered, had just got out of the 'big house'. I'm ashamed to say I stood back and watched as he dragged his girlfriend out by the hair. Initially I made a move to stop him but one of the students pulled me out of the way. She told me he was armed – with a gun. I was petrified. I didn't know what to do. I carried on with the lesson. After a while the girlfriend came back in. She'd been roughed up.

'Sorry 'bout that. He's a bastard.'

We got on with whatever we were doing like nothing had happened. Thankfully I never saw him again.

My white middle-class sensibilities were well and truly challenged in those first weeks. I quickly learnt my place. I never really thought about it at the time but I was a long way down the pecking order. I was just a teacher, and a white one at that. The only thing I had going for me was what I taught. I didn't hang around much in the early days either. I went in, taught a class and took off.

At the time I was acting and writing and preparing to direct *Black Cockatoos*. I had a three-year-old boy and a new baby girl. I had plenty to occupy my time and take my mind off Eora. It was the polar opposite to Tenterfield. I was discovering the benefits of the 'separation of powers'. There was teaching at Eora and my life in middle-class Balmain, which was metaphorically a long way from Redfern.

I'd never spent time in Redfern before. Even in the years 'between farms' when my family lived in Sydney, the only thing I knew about Redfern was the South Sydney Rabbitohs. Like most Sydneysiders I was afraid to go into Redfern. Like them I'd bought the propaganda. And like most propaganda, it was bullshit.

First principles

Teaching takes you into people's worlds in a way few other occupations can. You see a lot and hear a lot. Much of the time you are the proverbial fly on the wall. You can't help it – it's not like you're eavesdropping on purpose, you're just there. And you spend a lot of time with your classes. You get to know them well. It's often intense and you see sides to them that no one else sees. You see private moments when they're in their own worlds. They might be writing or thinking or even just daydreaming. You witness all sorts of interesting body language. Often you are all but invisible to your students. You might be there physically, you might even be giving a very interesting talk about something or other, but they are somewhere else entirely. It's hard to tell what anyone is thinking about and it's probably best not to ask.

The thing about teaching drama is that you ask people to expose themselves; to stand up in front of people and 'perform'. If you've had the stuffing knocked out of you, the idea of even standing up in front of people can be terrifying. If all your life your self-confidence has been undermined, it's unlikely you'll be confident about leaping to your feet and entertaining the troops. You'll probably want to hide.

Of course, there are performers who disappear into characters, who dress up and put on funny hats to escape the reality of their lives. But my class at Eora wasn't full of performers. It was full of people who were just 'doing a bit of drama'. One woman said to me:

'I didn't think I'd have to stand up in front of anyone.'

These were not acting students and certainly not actors. I was acutely aware of this and if I didn't handle it sensitively, then I'd be doing way more harm than good. It needed a 'softly softly' approach. I had no intention of exposing these people's vulnerabilities. They had been through enough. I had to re-evaluate the way I taught drama.

There was no single form or level or year; instead everyone was all jumbled together. The age range wasn't years, it was decades – from teenagers to 70-year-olds. There was an elderly woman who spoke with 'rounded vowels' and was almost as new to this world as I was. There was an older guy of indeterminate age who had lived ten lives and seen and done it all. While she was shy and retiring, he was the life of the party, especially if there was an audience. He loved an audience; she was terrified of one. She'd been educated; he could neither read nor write. They were like chalk and cheese.

There were several women in their thirties and forties who were there just to see what was happening. They had no particular ambitions. They loved being in class and focusing on things other than day-to-day living. I imagined one of them was there for the sole purpose of giving me a hard time. There were a couple of 20-year-olds with hopes of singing careers and dreams of stardom, and a teenager from the bush who was up for anything.

Among the men was a guy who was clearly heading for greater things; he was there to pick up some skills on the way and saw Eora as a stepping stone. He was very business-like and disciplined, and porous as a sponge. Another guy was tossing up between hairdressing and acting; I think he chose the former. One said he wanted to be an actor but, as far as I could tell, never learnt a line. Another did become one and worked with me on *Black Cockatoos*.

People came and went. Occasionally someone would come in and blow you off your feet and then you'd never see them again. It was pretty fluid. One thing was certain, each person required an individual approach.

The truth was, deep down I was scared of them all. Not physically scared, just scared that I wouldn't be able to help them or offer them anything of any value. I was afraid once more of being exposed as a fraud. I was afraid I'd do the wrong thing or say the wrong thing. Putting my foot in my mouth was a particular skill of mine. I prayed I wouldn't do it here.

I soon discovered that at Eora people took you at face value. They didn't care what you looked like or what you'd done or where you'd been. You were just who you were. They were interested in what you had to offer and that was it. If you were honest and true to yourself they cut you some slack. If you were full of shit they sent you packing. Playing the teacher wasn't going to get you very far. It was about what you did, not who you thought you were. There was nothing to hide behind. Pulling rank would get you nowhere because there was no rank to pull. Walking into class and delivering a few well-honed homilies about life and acting theory wouldn't exactly work either. What did they care about acting theory? And what could I possibly tell them about life?

'Be prepared' had been indelibly imprinted on my psyche from that first year at Tenterfield. So I was, and I was prepared to be flexible. I threw the drama textbook out the window and tried to think what would work for this particular group.

I decided to borrow an ice-breaking exercise a mate had told me about. I greeted my new class and told them I'd like them to stand up the front and say something about themselves.

'I'm not standing up there ...'

'None of your business.'

Not a great start. Then I had a bright idea.

'I'll go first.'

They couldn't have looked less interested.

'The idea is you stamp one foot and say your Christian name, then stamp the other one and say your surname. Like this.'

I demonstrated, stamping my left foot on the floor.

'Ned.'

I stamped the other foot.

'Manning.'

I'd never done this before in my life. I felt like a complete idiot. But I soldiered on. What was there to lose except my fast-disappearing dignity?

'Okay?'

Silence.

'Now, after you've introduced yourself, all you have to do is talk about yourself for a minute. It's not very long.'

It seemed like everyone had folded their arms and was looking right through me.

'Who'd like to go first?'

Silence. A bit of foot shuffling, a lot of eyes averted.

'I know, how about I go first?'

That worked. One or two glanced in my direction.

'Can someone time me?'

A cursory nod. Talk about fighting a losing battle.

'One minute.'

I held up my finger. I repeated the intro, just in case they'd forgotten who I was. Great start – what now? I had a minute to talk about myself. Normally this wouldn't be a problem. I could talk about myself till the cows came home, but this was different, this audience would be tough. What was I going to say?

'I was born in Coonabarabran. We kicked all the blackfellas off their land.'

Or: 'I went to a really posh school ...'

Even: 'I'm an actor. I starred in *Dead End Drive-In* ...'

Big deal.

I began to panic. A minute suddenly seemed a really long time. But I had no choice, I had to dive in. Big breath and away I went. I prattled on about where I lived, my family, my dog, the fact that I liked gardening and, for some reason, that I drove a Kombi and blah blah blah.

'That's a minute.' Pat held up his hand as if to say, 'That's enough.'

It was the longest minute of my life. The only thing I'd done was to give them a licence to fall on their face like I'd done.

'Who's next?'

They looked everywhere but in my direction.

'Come on, I did it.'

'You're an actor.'

Touché.

There was a bit of a Mexican stand-off. What was I going to do? I couldn't make them do what I wanted. Most of them were adults. There was no head teacher to send them to. There was no deten-tion to put them on. If they didn't want to move there was bugger all I could do about it. I was drowning. Again.

Thankfully, Edna took pity on me.

'I don't know what's wrong with you young people. You're here to learn aren't you?'

She got up and gave us a minute of her extraordinary life story. I wanted more. She fixed the rest of the class with a challenging gaze.

'Now, if I can do it, you can.'

She sat down and folded her arms.

Edna saved my bacon. She always grumbled about the youngies

in the class. When I say 'youngies' I'm referring to 30-year-olds. She didn't approve of their language or their manners. She used to mutter things about them under her breath. She gave me a serve one day for being a bit flippant. For a woman like her, this was a golden opportunity and she didn't want to squander a minute of it. She set the tone for the class and for the rest of my time at Eora. I am eternally grateful to her.

The second person to come to my rescue was the other old hand in the class. He too recognised the opportunity these guys had. He had little or no formal education; as far as opportunity was concerned he'd got the rough end of the pineapple. His life mirrored that of many Indigenous men of his generation and he wasn't going to look a gift horse in the mouth.

'Wake up to yourselves!'

He was an elder. They listened to him.

'He's the teacher.'

He'd often get stuck into the class for being disrespectful. He knew about authority and he'd had a lot to do with 'authorities'. It was strange being given this amount of respect from someone who had lived so much. What did I know compared to him?

He hopped up and off he went. I wasn't sure exactly what he was talking about – his 'yarns' were a bit like that. My greatest concern soon became how I was going to stop him after the minute had passed. It didn't look like he was going to stop. And he didn't. One of the others piped up.

'Come on, Pat. Sit down. You've had your turn.'

'But I'm only just warming up.'

Pat was the life and soul of the party, and the heart of Eora.

One by one they got up and offered glimpses of their lives. They awakened me to a whole new world. I heard about pretending you weren't black to get a job; I heard about *discovering* you were black; I heard about being a gay black man; I heard about pride and dreams – acting dreams, singing dreams, writing dreams.

I sat there listening with my jaw on the floor. I had tears in my eyes. I had stumbled into a world so far from any I knew that I might as well have stumbled onto Mars. Yet it was in Redfern, in the heart of the biggest city in the country and less than ten kilometres from where I lived. How could I be so ignorant of a world that was so geographically close to mine?

By the time everyone had their minute, we were all exhausted. It was pretty confronting. No one quite knew what to say or what to do. Then Pat broke the ice with a joke. We all laughed, some of us might have even cried. It didn't matter. We were away.

Once we'd got our breath back I asked them what they wanted to do, what they wanted out of my drama classes. After all I was there for them, not to follow some syllabus. They told me they wanted to learn how to audition. There was a bit of work for Koori actors at the time and they wanted to be able to put their hand up for whatever was on offer.

Why not?

At the end of the lesson I handed out some scripts I'd photocopied: speeches, short monologues taken from classic plays by Arthur Miller, Tennessee Williams, Sam Shepherd, David Williamson and Samuel Beckett, pieces that covered a wide range of life experiences without being too specific. I asked them to learn them or at least be familiar with them. I figured a good way to start would be to work on some basic acting skills using great writing. I also told them not to worry about accents. They all assured me they were excited about learning the pieces and the lesson finished on a pretty good note. I was looking forward to the next one.

When I turned up the next week for class I noticed that the bulk of those who came to the first class were back for more, along with one or two new faces. We got straight into it. One by one I called them up to deliver their monologues. They were hesitant, even apologetic. Most of them hadn't learnt their lines but at least they were there. My notes from that lesson included comments like:

Nothing learnt but here
Nothing learnt but preparing folio, death in family, moving
Nothing learnt but interpreted piece brilliantly
Audition piece from video
Piece from play currently performing
Nothing learnt – interpreted piece brilliantly

I was quickly coming to terms with a very complex set of circumstances. For a start, most of these people had never done anything like this before in their lives. I was asking them to run a marathon before they could walk. It was further complicated when I started letting them off the hook. Their response was to get stuck into me, especially Pat. He didn't beat around the bush.

'You're the bloody teacher, you make us do it! Don't listen to any bloody excuses.'

They *wanted* me to push them. They didn't have time to learn to walk. Most were middle-aged and older, they had been denied opportunity most of their lives and now that they had it they were going to grab it with both hands. My challenge was that they all wanted something different and they all had very different skills levels.

This would have been hard enough if everyone in my class went home to the same living conditions as their white counterparts. But the demands of their day-to-day lives were far more complicated than most white Australians ever encounter. Even finding somewhere to live was loaded for Indigenous Australians. They often had complex family situations to deal with alongside the difficulties of living in the big smoke. And living in Sydney has never been cheap.

We went very slowly and very carefully. I took each person through their pieces and helped them make some sense of them. It went pretty well and they were incredibly receptive. My notes from the next class read:

First time, nervous, no eye contact
Excellent preparation, good reading
Learnt piece, very good when not worrying about words
Hadn't learnt piece, very natural, nervous, needs confidence
Great understanding of meaning, learning words slowly

We were making progress. It was very difficult for most of them and they found performing confronting. That is, everyone except Pat. He loved it. He would have spent all day on his piece if I'd let him. The trouble with Pat was getting him off the stage. But the others needed to be coaxed gently to their feet. Even though I insisted they weren't being judged, they hated everyone looking at them. They would have done their pieces happily if it were just for me – it was their people they worried about. Who cared what I thought?

Edna dreaded the performing side of drama. She loved the preparation and knew her piece backwards. She just didn't want to do it in public. But she wouldn't give up. As hard as it was, as terrified as she was, she kept pushing herself. I told her it didn't matter if she didn't perform. It did though, to her. She had a mountain to climb and she was going to climb it. It was gut-wrenching to watch her put herself through this agony. Week after week she'd get up, forget her lines and sit down again. A few times she was so nervous she couldn't even start. But nothing was going to stop her. She'd take one step forward and three backwards but she never gave up. It was a matter of pride.

Towards the end of the term she got up and made her way to the front of the class. She handed me the script. She was shaking.

She wanted me to prompt her. I tried to offer some encouragement but she didn't need anything from me. This was about conquering her mountain. And she did. When she finished the class went wild. Everyone jumped to their feet and gave her a standing ovation. She was as proud as punch. It was great.

The rest of the class sat somewhere between Pat and Edna. Some went ahead in leaps and bounds; they got on top of the words and they stood up and delivered them confidently. Others stumbled through them but were happy with that. They had achieved whatever it was they wanted. Only one person procrastinated: Annie. She was also the hardest to read. Even though she had raised a young family, in class she was like a naughty kid, always giving me a hard time and wise-cracking. It was like she was making up for lost time.

Annie wouldn't get up. She kept making excuses. I tried to encourage her but the rest of the class was getting impatient – they wanted her to get on with it so they could have a go. I told her to get a move on. She glared at me.

'You know what you can do with your lines?'

Then she stormed out.

I thought I'd seen the end of her but she was back the next week and her performance was word-perfect. When she finished she looked at me as if to say, 'Stick that up your jumper!' I grinned at her – I was stoked. Deep down she was too.

The 'term' ended and we all felt a great sense of achievement. We'd had good attendances and we'd got some work done. I decided I'd be back for more.

I did some acting work towards the end of 1989; things like *A Country Practice* and *G.P.* as well as some film work. I was also directing *Black Cockatoos* and writing a new play, so I was unavailable to work at Eora for the rest of the year.

Excursions

In 1990 I returned with more of an idea of what Eora was about. I had been through my baptism of fire and I felt more confident about what might be possible. That first year had been about laying foundations. Now we were on our way. The place was changing. There was still the same positive energy but you could tell that everyone wanted more; they wanted to push the envelope and see what happened. I was more than happy to help.

The bulk of the class of '89 had returned, plus some welcome additions. We were getting to know each other pretty well and we were starting to trust each other, which meant we could take more risks and be more adventurous. I didn't feel as though I was treading on eggshells anymore. We began classes with warm-up exercises, something that would have been unimaginable 12 months before. We did improv, character work, scene work. We did theatre sports and play readings. We got stuck in. There were no more comings and goings either. The same group was there for every class; they were on time and prepared to work.

I gave out more scenes for them to work on. Now that I knew them I could fashion the material I gave them to suit their needs, interests and abilities. We worked on the scenes and came up with the idea of bringing them all together into a show. The group had enormous pride in the performance levels they had reached and they wanted to share this achievement with their brothers and sisters at Eora. There'd been heaps of music concerts and art exhibitions and they wanted their turn to show how far they had travelled.

We created a premise for the show. They were to be a bunch of travelling players, like the ones in *Hamlet*. This bunch of players were all blackfellas and they were performing excerpts from the classics, including Shakespeare. Not a lot of Indigenous performers got the chance to play classical roles at that time; most of the roles they were cast in involved being abused or tossed in the slammer. They were always playing victims so what we were doing was pretty special. It was years before an Indigenous actor would be cast as Othello.

We combined the text work with music; there always had to be music. It was eclectic, combining traditional and contemporary, along with songs and even a bit of opera. We also built a moment into the show when Pat told a 'yarn'. His yarns were a bit of a moveable feast and varied in length, usually from long to even longer. The 'hook' was applied by a few of the female characters who would gently move him off if he built up too much steam.

I wrote some bridging dialogue to bring it all together. The focus was on performance skills and stagecraft. None of these guys had been on stage before, or, if they had, not since school. It was a big call for a bunch of adults who weren't necessarily used to being the centre of attention, but they were united in their desire to prove to one and all that they could rise to the challenge.

Teamwork was crucial and being supportive came naturally to the Kooris I met at Eora. These guys would crawl over cut glass for each other. After rehearsals and performances it is customary for the director to give 'notes': feedback on aspects of the production. If I gave a note about helping each other when someone forgot a line, they would leap at the chance. When Pat was telling his yarn he would have their full attention. They never needed a note about listening. They were all ears.

They immediately understood characters like Olive from *Summer of the Seventeenth Doll* and Linda from *Death of a Salesman*, women who did it tough, who were uncompromising and fought for their dignity. They could draw on a wellspring of life experiences to bring these characters to life.

The problem arose when they were in the spotlight. Unlike a lot of performers, they weren't obsessed with themselves. They weren't worried about being 'discovered' or about what everyone thought of them individually. They weren't seeking my approval either, so I never heard the usual actors' laments:

'Was I okay?'

'I was a bit off tonight.'

'How was it?

'I know. I was shit tonight.'

'Did they like me?'

I don't think they ever talked about themselves in that way. In fact, I often wished they were a little more into themselves and that they would take the focus when the excerpts demanded it. Monologues by definition throw the performer onto centre stage; they become the focus of everyone's attention. But if learning the words was hard enough, stepping into the limelight – away from the 'family' – was almost a bridge too far.

As their teacher I had to help them to get where they wanted to go. I had to give them the tools they needed to face a very big personal challenge – to cross the footlights into the audience – and to be able to do it the same way performance after performance. Learning those skills took years but these guys didn't have years; they wanted to do their monologues *now*. They wanted to extend themselves, to prove something to themselves. In a funny way I could see that it didn't really have a lot to do with performing in the traditional sense. It was something more important than that. Their need was so personal, so individual and so deep-seated. It wasn't my place to ask why they were putting themselves through this or even why they were doing drama in the first place.

I wasn't a counsellor and I certainly wasn't into psychodrama. I was a teacher. I focused on entrances and exits, on where they might stand or how they might angle their bodies. On how they used their voices. I was always at them to turn up the volume. I encouraged them to isolate their thoughts and to play them one at a time. I pushed them to think about what they were saying. I might highlight certain words that needed consideration or emphasis. And to keep their minds on the job, to focus.

Unlike in most schools, there weren't any assessments. Nor was there, thankfully, any marking. The students set their own pass mark; not me, not the Board of Studies, not anyone. Maybe that's what I really loved about teaching at Eora. You never had to give a student who had tried really hard a bad mark. You never had to argue for students to get rewarded for their efforts even if they went over time. You never, ever had to humiliate a student who had made a mistake or hadn't done the work or was scared. And, there was no bloody ranking.

The tricky thing was to work out exactly what their personal pass mark was. Each person had an individual goal. Some really wanted to discover if they could become actors. Others were push-ing through personal barriers by getting up in front of an audience. Others were just letting their hair down and having fun. Pat gave himself an A+ every time. I've never seen anyone get such a kick out of being part of a show. He loved it and everyone loved him. For him it was a treasured gift just being there; he knew it and he relished it. More than once he confided in me that it was his 'second or maybe third coming'.

It was more complicated with the others. I had to try and work out what they wanted and often it was hidden behind bravado or cheek or 'attitude' – or, on one or two occasions, outright aggression. Sometimes they voiced aspirations that were clearly beyond their grasp. More often, they kept it to themselves.

The biggest challenge was to inspire confidence in their own abilities. Underneath the bravado was a good deal of fear. And it was ingrained fear, the fear only someone who has been undermined since birth could ever understand. I would often forget to consider what emotional state a student might be in: what crisis had exploded in their lives? What physical stress were they under? What emotional stress? It's easy to do when you're full steam ahead trying to rally the troops. If I had to be careful never to give someone a task that was beyond them, I also had to be careful not to undermine their confidence by patronising them. It was a fine line to tread.

'You all have the ability if you trust yourselves, throw away self-doubt and self-consciousness, and concentrate.'

I can't believe I said that but I did. It's amazing I'm still here to tell the story, but that's teaching – often your enthusiasm can lead you to say and do things which, later, you can only shake your head at.

Sometimes my notes were met with open hostility. When I told young Cindy to lift her energy, she glared at me. It was a real 'fuck off' moment. But I kept at it and her energy in performance went through the roof.

The students at Eora would always come up with the best lines during notes. After one disastrous rehearsal, Bettina made the immortal observation:

'We're all gonna get somewhere. All we gotta do is learn our lines.'

She was talking about herself. Bettina had forgotten her lines. She'd 'dried' – that is, she couldn't remember where she was or what she was doing. It's a dreadful feeling. Her solution was to collapse onto Jan's shoulder and shake her head. Everyone laughed. Bettina was a natural comic. Then the light bulb went on:

'That's it!'

She straightened herself up and continued playing Olive as though nothing had happened. It brought the house down. I gave her a note that she didn't have to tell the audience when she'd forgotten a line!

In the lead-up to the show their run was, to be honest, terrible. They forgot lines, missed entrances and exits, broke up laughing when they made mistakes, you name it, they did it. The best I could offer was the note:

Lose negative thoughts before, during and after.

Geoff was more to the point. He was angry with them.

'To think you can be so confident!'

I was secretly cheering him on as he lit into them, but it was a strange role-reversal with the students playing 'bad cop', telling each other a few home truths, while I played the 'good cop' searching for positives. It's not that I didn't push them, but I knew that if they were going to succeed with this project, they had to feel good about themselves. There was no point in me blowing up at them; instead my task was to make them feel valued. As I discovered, that is the key to good teaching. That's why my asking 'Woody' Forrester what he was doing tied to the roof at Tenterfield was so wrong. In trying to curry favour with the rest of the class by using his nickname, I undermined him. And I paid for it.

Besides, I had enough on my hands without blowing up at them. It nearly killed me trying to get Annie to bow at the end of the show. She was so relieved about getting there she just wanted to bolt. The idea of receiving applause and curtain calls was foreign to all those guys. I told them it was a way of thanking the audience for watching. But it didn't matter what I said – when the last line was delivered, they fell in a heap. And that was just the dress rehearsal.

Performance day was fast approaching and we still didn't have a title. I pleaded with them.

'Come on, who's going to take responsibility for the title?'

'Not this little black duck!' one of them piped up.

We had our title. *Not This Little Black Duck*. It was perfect.

The atmosphere in the foyer before the show at Eora was pretty low-key. The whole student body plus friends and family were there. I don't think anyone knew what to expect; everyone just sort of milled around waiting for it to start. I'm not sure what they made of it but when it was over they were very generous – they clapped and cheered and there were a few wolf-whistles. The cast bowed and skedaddled. When they emerged from behind the hastily arranged backdrop there was a sense of relief. From the audience the overwhelming sentiment was one of slightly bemused pride. It really didn't matter if it was good or bad, or if they understood what was happening on stage, or even if they liked Shakespeare. All that mattered was that it happened. It was done. And, for all of those students, it was a personal milestone.

And it was just the beginning.

The Koori grapevine spreads far and wide. We received an invitation to take *Not This Little Black Duck* to the north coast of New South Wales. A couple of our students came from the area and everyone was very excited. We got a bit of funding from somewhere, booked trains and accommodation, and off we went. Things happened like that at Eora: quickly and unexpectedly.

It was an excursion with a difference. It was a cultural exchange of sorts, where we would see some traditional stuff and, in return, we would show the people in the Nambucca Heads area our stuff.

It was pretty exciting. Not only had we managed to get a performance up, we were now taking it on the road.

This was my first outing with my students and the first time I'd spent any length of time with them outside Eora. Apart from what we did in class, they didn't know a lot about me and I didn't know much about them. We didn't really know each other as people; they knew me as a teacher, I knew them as students. This excursion was to change all that.

You learn a lot about people when you travel with them outside their comfort zones. When I first went to Eora I never dreamt I'd end up travelling with a bunch of students. At first I wasn't all that keen on going but I couldn't resist the possibilities. And I couldn't let them down – if I didn't go there would be no excursion.

That's the thing about teaching. You get sucked in by the job. It's addictive. You see your students growing and you spend every waking hour dreaming up ways of continuing that growth. You see limitless possibilities. You think about how you can extend them. You try to work out what you can do for the ones who are struggling. You become obsessed with them. Your partners get sick of you banging on about them. They consume your life. That's why you can't quantify the hours teachers work. They never really 'clock off'. Without any change in pay rate, my two four-hour classes morphed into four 24-hour days.

From the moment we assembled at Central Station I could see a definite change in the pecking order. I might have been the teacher but I certainly wasn't in charge. Pat and Annie assumed a leadership role and the rest of us followed orders. Annie was very good at giving orders. I did a lot of listening and observing. The parameters couldn't have been more different from every other excursion I'd been on. For a start I was on an excursion with adults. I still felt I was responsible for them, but not in the same way as I would have been if they were kids. For a start, smoking wasn't prohibited and a few of us had a beer or two together.

We got the train to Macksville and were met at the station by some members of the local Indigenous community. They showed us around and drove us to our accommodation at the aptly named The Last Resort. The next few days were taken up with performances and cultural exchanges. I often wondered what the locals made of the white dude who was tagging along with the Eora gang. Apart from performances where I did have a role to play, I was pretty much superfluous.

On the last day we travelled by bus to Bowraville. I'd never heard of Bowraville; in the 19th century it had been the epicentre of the Nambucca Valley with booming timber and diary industries. Like many country towns, it fell into decline as the industries fell away. We came across a tiny town nestled in the mountains. We were there because the Indigenous community made up nearly 40 per cent of its population. There were vestiges of its former glory but it had clearly seen better days. There was a very strange vibe in the place – you could sense it the moment you got off the bus. It seemed deserted. There was almost no one on the main street.

I went into the local pub to find out where the hall was. It was like walking into the scene from *Gorillas in the Mist* when Dian Fossey stumbles into a bar full of desperados at the edge of civilisation. On the wall was the weirdest and most violent painting I have ever seen. It was a depiction of the 'old days'. The bullocky days. It was very primitive – it could have been painted by a kid in kindergarten were it not for the subject matter. There were bullocks with blood spurting from their severed heads. Fountains of blood. There were men with axes chopping down everything in sight. It was very disturbing.

I asked for directions.

'What do you wanna go there for?'

'We're doing a show.'

'Who?'

'We're up from Sydney.'

'The big smoke.'

'Yeah.'

'What sorta show?'

'Oh, it's a kind of show … bits of Shakespeare and stuff.'

'Shakespeare?'

'Yes. And classics.'

'Oh …'

'You ought to come and have a look.'

'Shakespeare? I don't think so.'

'Look, I'm sorry but we need to find the hall.'

'You mean the Bowra Theatre? Bit run-down now, she is.'

'That's okay.'

'Used to be a picture theatre.'

His mate came to my rescue.

'He don't want a bloody history lesson. It's down the road there.'

He pointed out a derelict old hall.

'Got a key?'

'I think we're meeting someone there. Thanks.'

I tried to escape.

'Who'd you say you were again?'

'We're from Eora. The Aboriginal Centre for Visual and Performing Arts.'

'What's that?'

'In Redfern.'

'Coons?'

What did he say?

'Doin' Shakespeare?'

I made a faltering recovery.

'That's … that's right.'

'Fair dinkum?'

'Thanks for the directions.'

I would have been stunned by this exchange in any context, but given what we'd been through together I was completely floored by their barefaced racism. Bowraville was clearly a racist town, which was odd given that nearly half the town were black. I learnt that in the 'good old days' when the theatre was flourishing it was also segregated. The local Indigenous community had to enter the theatre through a different door from the local whites, they bought their tickets at a different booth and they were given the worst seats in a cordoned-off area. Apartheid. That's why it was a port of call on the 1965 Freedom Ride.

While I was getting directions my mob had jumped off the bus and were laughing and mucking around. They were in high spirits. The trip had been a huge success. This was our last performance and they were all pumped.

'What's up with you?'

'Nothing. The hall's over there. Let's get going.'

They took the piss. They knew I was upset about something but I never told them what it was.

Rudimentary would be an understatement to describe the theatre. We set up and began a run-through. It was necessary to do this because everywhere we played was different, but some of the students didn't see the point. There was a bit of tension.

'Just bloody do it.'

It was the first time I'd lost my cool with them. They thought I was homesick, missing the kids and my comfy whitefella lifestyle. But I was still blown away by the exchange I'd had in the pub. I was worried about who was going to turn up. I was really uncomfortable in this place. I wanted to get the show over and done with and get back to Nambucca.

The stage didn't have any lighting. How were they going to be seen? A mate I'd run into in Macksville and who had come along for the ride suggested we get hold of some lamps.

'Where from?'

I made my way back to the pub and borrowed a couple of reading lights.

'Make sure you bring 'em back.'

When we discovered the switches didn't work my mate came up with the ingenious idea of pulling the cords out of the socket to turn the lights off and sticking them back in to turn them on. He sat in front of one power point, I took my place in front of the other and we operated the lights manually. It kind of worked.

Show time was fast approaching, as was nightfall. There was no sign of anyone coming. Oh well. We'd just do it and get the hell out of there.

I asked our liaison guy if he thought anyone would show up. He shrugged his shoulders. I think I bludged a rollie off him and went outside for a smoke. I wasn't a smoker. In the short history of *Not This Little Black Duck* this was the first time I'd been nervous. I just didn't know what to expect.

A few people started wandering in. Local Kooris. I chatted to a few of them. They were pretty unforthcoming. Then more trickled in. Every time I was about to give the signal for the show to kick off the door would open and another few would appear. Before long the place was half full. There were lots of kids running around. Suddenly the atmosphere changed. I went backstage.

'There's people here. Lots of them.'

Someone had a peek through the curtain.

'Jeez, it's nearly full.'

They were all starting to get nervous. The other shows we'd done were pretty low-key. School groups and small communities. This was different. This was a proper theatre and it was filling up. I tried to calm their nerves.

'You'll be right. Just focus on what you're doing.'

Some of them were getting antsy. A few little spats blew up.

'Okay. We're going to start. Go for it guys.'

As I made my way to my power socket I noticed the theatre was now full. There were even people up the back, leaning against the wall. Then I realised who they were: the guys from the pub. The back wall was lined with whitefellas while in the body of the theatre, in the best seats, was the local Koori community. I plugged in the lamp and we were away.

'Two households, both alike in dignity, in fair Verona ...'

You could have heard a pin drop.

It was amazing. I was captivated. I nearly missed my cue to yank out the light for a blackout. If the show at Eora had been groundbreaking this was earth-shattering. The atmosphere was electric. The audience were on the edge of their seats. Their eyes were like saucers. The guys up the back weren't leaning anymore – they were pushing forward so as to not miss a word. The odd kid was still running around but apart from that the students had the audience in the palm of their hands. There was rapturous applause after each monologue. They laughed at all our jokes.

It was magic.

I'd never experienced anything like it. The students lifted their performances to places they'd never been and the audience responded in kind. Pat brought the house down. He had to be dragged off as he waved his hat at adoring fans. I think he might have even done a little jig. Annie showed performance skills she'd never shown before. Bettina was as funny as a circus. Cindy sang like a bird. Jan remembered her words.

When it was over there was a standing ovation. The noise was deafening. The cast took their curtain call. They raised their arms in triumph. They bowed as one. They were so pumped they could have floated back to The Last Resort.

No one left. The students mingled with their new fans. People were shaking their heads in amazement. The Koori pride was palpable. Even the guys from the pub were blown away.

'I never knew coons could do that kind of thing.'

'You mean Aborigines?'

'That was pretty bloody amazing.'

'You liked it?'

'You got me lights?'

'Real eye-opener that was.'

I was stoked. We had a cup of tea, said our farewells and made our way back to the bus. It was like we'd won the grand final. Everyone was on an incredible high. The bus was rockin' all the way back to The Last Resort.

The trip to Macksville marked a turning point in our relationship as teacher and students. The Bowraville experience had been the kind of positive reinforcement every teacher dreams of. Everything I'd been banging on about suddenly had some credibility. They could join the dots. They had experienced the potential of their subject instead of hearing a whole lot of warm and fuzzy anecdotes about it from their teacher. Their hard work had paid off.

The whole class from youngest to oldest had experienced a kind of catharsis. It was astonishing. All the way home they talked excitedly about the possibilities that lay before them. They had gained the sort of confidence that only success can garner. When I'd first tried to get Annie up in front of the class, she'd folded her arms and refused.

'Fuck off. I'm not getting up there.'

She had more than challenged me – she'd palmed me off. Now she had not only got up there, she'd got up there and held an audience spellbound. She had conquered some personal demons and caught a glimpse of what she might be able to achieve in the future. After her triumph, she was grinning like a Cheshire cat.

Excursions open eyes. They take students outside comfort zones and, by exposing them to unfamiliar worlds, force them to reflect on their own insularity. They enable them to make new friends. And they are fun.

For teachers they are an enormous responsibility and they're hard work. In New South Wales, for instance, when you want to take kids on an excursion you have to organise your own 'cover'. That means you have to ask a colleague to take your classes for you on top of their own classes. Asking favours like this puts pressure on relationships. Once upon a time the school would organise relief for you. What's more, there's enough paperwork involved in organising an excursion these days to make a tax auditor baulk. Yet excursions are, without question, the key to broadening perspectives and expanding horizons.

Armed with new-found confidence and self-belief, the students at Eora sailed into their next project: a production of *Little Shop of Horrors*. It was the first full-on production Eora had undertaken. It was directed by the music teacher and I was called in to help with performance. My notes reflected how far they had come. For example, I was giving them notes using their character names; they started identifying with the characters they were playing. This was a massive step for them.

> *Seymour let go: more enthusiasm*
> *During freeze be aware of expressions, esp. Audrey. Keep it light, Audrey*

I was able to ask for levels of performance that were inconceivable a year earlier, which shows just how much they had learned.

> *Pace – cues quicker*
> *Listen to the lyrics, i.e. the words are telling us the story*

*Girls with fans share in Audrey's dream, i.e. listen to words and
act appropriately*
The song is called 'Some Fun Now'. Have fun singing it!
FOR FUCK'S SAKE DON'T LOOK BORED!!!

If I'd spoken to them like that a year ago they would have
walked out. That's what trust leads to: being able to call it like it
is. When you're on a roll with a class you might use 'inappropriate'
language but that's because you are so into the work you forget to
censor yourself. And guess what? No one gives a shit! It's a wonderful contradiction that plagues the teaching profession: we're meant
to wear straightjackets, but wearing them stops you from doing
anything.

Little Shop of Horrors went off. The audience went ape shit.
They laughed and clapped and roared their approval. The students
finished the year on an incredible high. They deserved it.

High distinctions

When we got together in December to plan the following year we were buoyed by a new sense of possibility. After the *Not This Little Black Duck* tour, the sky seemed to be the only limit. My notes from this meeting include references to:

<u>An Aboriginal Play</u>
   script: Bettina
   funding: Annie
   venue: Nathan

<u>Theatre Sports in Schools</u>
   funding: Joni, Ned

<u>Documentaries</u>
   funding: Ned, SBS, ABC

<u>Community Workshop</u>
   funding: Bettina, Ned

<u>Radio Plays</u>
   script: Bettina

<u>Established Plays</u>
   funding: Rosie

We had follow-up meetings, allocated jobs for everyone over the break and set a date to meet again in the new year. My part-time job was becoming more and more full-time.

That's what happens to teachers: they are seduced by possibility. They swear they won't be but their very nature makes them easy targets. They are always looking at ways to extend their students and almost never consider the kind of commitment it will require from them. That's just not in the nature of most teachers. However if they continue to have roadblocks put in front of them, they will eventually be discouraged.

I have often wondered if there was some perverted strategy in place to force teachers to abandon exciting projects in the name of mediocrity. It sounds absurd but if you've ever worked in a school and tried to do something outside the square, you'd know exactly what I am talking about.

Why doesn't the department encourage true initiative? Why are they so obsessed with committees, committees and more committees? Do they think professionalism requires endless meetings and reams of new jargon?

Thankfully there were no such roadblocks at Eora. The place was blossoming before our eyes. In every subject there was a determination to mine whatever possibilities lay undiscovered. TAFE had taken over, expanded its reach and formalised some of the teaching, but the spirit of the place was unchanged.

The students were getting work outside Eora. They formed a 'theatre sports' team and called it The Redfern Mob. Theatre sports was an improvisational team game played at the Belvoir St Theatre. The Redfern Mob killed 'em! They were cast in educational videos, conducted workshops, did some TV and worked on films. Things were happening and at the beginning of 1991, we were ready to rock and roll.

I asked Ernie Dingo to come to the class to inspire the students, and inspire them he did. He was way more forceful than I'd ever dare to be. It may have been his first time at Eora, but Ernie was one of them. He told them they needed to get off their arses and tell their stories. I could never have presumed to tell them something like that. I wasn't a blackfella, I was their teacher. There was a clear line of demarcation. They told me what they wanted to do and I helped them achieve it. That's the way it worked.

Ernie gave us the motivation we needed. If the students came up with some stories, I could help collate them and shape them into a show we could perform on stage. This would feed into the two disciplines I was now teaching: acting and writing.

Some of the students were into writing. In my classes I was encouraging them to write all sorts of stuff, including their own stories. I even helped Pat write his, essentially acting as his scribe. It was an amazing yarn.

Creating an original show seemed like a really good idea – a natural progression from the work we'd done. The response to *Not This Little Black Duck* and *Little Shop of Horrors* had given them enormous confidence about performing in front of an audience and they were more than up for a challenge of this nature. There were plenty of volunteers to write the show. Naturally it would need music too; you couldn't imagine a show about blackfellas without it. The students had been writing lots of poetry, much of it quite beautiful, so writing lyrics was not going to be a problem. And there were plenty of budding musos at Eora. Scott Saunders of DIG fame was teaching there and he volunteered to help arrange the music.

I was very excited about this new initiative. With Scott and I working only in the background it was a perfect teaching tool. I would be like the woodwork teacher looking on and, from time to time, gently advising his charges as they crafted their pieces. After *Not This Little Black Duck* I was acutely aware that I needed to be less hands-on, which was why I only helped with *Little Shop of*

Horrors as a kind of acting coach. My role was to empower and to impart skills. They'd perform it at Eora and it would be a natural step on our journey.

As an exercise I suggested to the class that I film them in Redfern Park 'spinning a few yarns'. Whatever they could come up with; no pressure, no big deal. The idea was to get some experience in front of a camera. Wim Wenders was going to be making *Until the End of the World* in Australia and the producer had asked me to help with casting Indigenous performers. By default my job description was expanding to include (unpaid) casting consultant!

We headed off to Redfern Park and began filming. The first few were a mixed bag: some told jokes, others talked about themselves without giving too much away. It was all a bit aimless. Good acting experience I suppose, but the material was pretty thin. When it was Annie's turn she was typically brusque.

'What am I gonna talk about?'

'I don't know. Anything.'

'I don't like cameras.'

'Come on, Annie. We haven't got all day.'

'Oh all right, let's get it over with.'

I pointed the camera in her direction and away she went.

'I'm gonna tell you a story about my sister. She was a real character my sister. She was the life and soul of the party. She was a real happy kid. She got on with everyone. She was always laughing and clowning around. So one day when we were walking home from school and she was quiet for once, I knew something was up. I asked what was wrong. She wouldn't tell me. She told me I was "too little". I wouldn't understand. She musta been eight or even nine. She was sooo old!'

Annie laughed. Her eyes were sparkling. I thought how much the camera loved her. It's funny how the camera loves some people.

'That night when we were having tea she asked our parents

what a nigger was. They tried to brush it off, like anything to do with black people. When something came on the telly about Martin Luther King or blacks in America, they changed the channel. They didn't want to know about it. They didn't want *us* to know about it. My sis, she wouldn't take no for an answer. She kept nagging at them no matter what they tried to do to change the subject.'

I had no idea where this story was heading.

'She wore 'em down but. She was a bugger. Once she got a fix on something she was like a dog with a bloody bone. She just wouldn't let go. Eventually they gave up and told her. I wasn't meant to be listening but I was hiding behind the door.

'"A nigger is a black person. Happy?"

'My dad went back to whatever he was doing. My mum asked her, "Why do you want to know?"

'"Nothing."

'That was the end of it. Or so they thought.

'When we went to bed she didn't want to talk. She *always* wanted to talk. She could talk the legs off a chair. But not tonight. She covered her head with a pillow. She was sobbing, crying. I asked what was wrong. She wouldn't say anything. She was trying to protect me. I got into bed with her and gave her a cuddle. I'd never seen her that upset.

'The next morning I woke up and she wasn't there. I freaked out. Maybe she'd run away. She'd joked about it before. I jumped out of bed and ran into the bathroom. There she was, standing in front of the mirror, trying to scrub her skin off. Her face was red raw.'

The camera started shaking in my hands. Tears were welling in my eyes. Annie looked straight down the barrel. She wasn't smiling anymore. That cheeky grin of hers had disappeared.

'When those kids had called her a nigger, she didn't know what they were talking about. We'd never even heard the word, let alone known what it meant. We certainly didn't know it was meant to be an insult. We were little kids in primary school. We called each other names all the time.'

There was a calm about Annie that was unnerving.

'We didn't even know we were *black*. We were dark-skinned but we never really thought about it. It wasn't a big deal. At that age skin-colour didn't seem to be any more of an issue than red hair or freckles.'

How could they not know they were black? Aboriginal? She had a point about learnt behaviour though. I thought about how kids in kindergarten hold hands with each other no matter what their sex. Then she drove the point home.

'You were taught racial prejudice. It didn't come naturally.'

Annie could intuit that I didn't get it. Or maybe she could see the camera wobbling all over the place. She knew I was struggling.

'Our parents were white. Well, they weren't really our parents. They were our adoptive parents. Although they didn't really adopt us. We were given to them when we were taken away.'

By now the tears were streaming down my face. I could hardly hold the camera still. God knows what the footage looked like. I never saw it. And I'll never, ever forget that moment. It blew me away. Annie was always taking the piss, giving me a hard time. She was the driving force behind our class. But she wasn't at all forthcoming about herself. In fact, even this story hadn't been about her – it had been about her sister. She told me the story of her sister and in telling it laid bare the shocking reality of the Stolen Generations.

Of course I knew a little about the Stolen Generations but not a lot. I'd never been exposed to the truth; certainly nothing as revelatory as this. It was a dreadful, heartbreaking story. When she finished, she looked at me.

'What's up with you?'

I couldn't say anything. I mumbled something about the camera running out of tape and we began making our way back to school. I was shattered. I'd expected a nice little outing in the park and I got a kick in the guts. I felt equal measures of shame and disgust. Funny that blackfellas use the word 'shame' all the time. It should be our word, especially when dealing with our past. I'd spent three years at Tenterfield and I hadn't learnt a lot about Indigenous Australia, despite making heaps of Koori friends. How could I have been so ignorant? It was embarrassing.

Teaching is revealing in what it tells you about yourself and your students, but it is also emotionally exhausting. Teachers feel for their students. Teachers are givers, they give themselves to their classes. And whether they like it or not they become emotionally involved with them. They share their joy and their pain in equal measures. It's impossible to clock-off when you are worried about another human being, and that's what your students are: human beings. I know that sounds obvious but the way some people talk about them you'd think they were statistics.

The next time I met with my class I told them that they had their story. When I told them about what Annie had said, without going into detail, I discovered that Annie wasn't the only member of my class affected by the Stolen Generations. Everyone had a story about it; everyone had either been taken away themselves or had a relative who'd been taken away.

The dynamic in the class had shifted immeasurably. I was now a privileged interloper. I sat there taking notes, listening to the stories and wondering what sort of country we were living in. Not the least because if someone like me, with connections in the Indigenous world, didn't know about this stuff what chance was there that the wider community would?

One thing I did know was that we had to tell this story and they were the ones who were going to write it. It wasn't my place to write it – I was adamant about that. I knew all about 'appropriation' of Indigenous art by whitefellas and there was no way I was going to get caught up in that mess. I'd help my class put it all together but they would be the ones telling the story.

Our classes became workshops where we threw around ideas. The improvisations were incredibly powerful – at times they were so painful they were almost unwatchable. There was a level of truth in them that was extraordinary. Talk about being emotionally accessible! Once they got started these guys didn't know how to hold back. And now they were developing the skills to translate these raw emotions into performance. I knew, once we got a script, they could get on stage and bring it off. We set a performance date.

Every class we'd do more exploring. That was one of the advantages about improvising a curriculum: you could go with the flow. We laughed a lot and, of course, there were a few tears. It was all very productive but there weren't any words on the page. As much as they insisted they would go home and write scenes, they'd turn up to the next lesson empty-handed. We mapped out a potential story line for the first few scenes. Still no words, nothing to work on.

I started to get a bit agitated. This was a huge undertaking. We were taking on material that was explosive. Nothing had appeared on any of our stages about the Stolen Generations and this work would draw a lot of attention. We needed to get it right. Scott was writing some great music and putting together a band; although most of them had never played in public before, let alone in a stage show, their songs were coming together. All we needed was the play.

It looked like we were going to start serious rehearsals without a script. We had improvised the scenes we wanted to investigate to within an inch of themselves but I didn't think they had the experience to improvise a whole show. Nor did they. We had reached a stalemate.

I asked them if they were serious about this project. I told them they couldn't afford to go backwards – they had to come up with something, anything. It got pretty heated. I was no longer the politically correct, shrinking violet of a few years ago. The people who were meant to be writing the show wouldn't look me in the eye. There were endless excuses but I wasn't buying any of them. Something was going on. Eventually someone blurted out:

'Why don't you just write it?'

'Because ...'

Silence.

'You know why.'

They looked at me. I almost pleaded with them.

'You wrote *Not This Little Black Duck*.'

'Don't give me the shits. That was different. It was an exercise.'

'It was good.'

Pat was getting restless.

'What's wrong with youse?'

He was about to deliver one of his unique pep talks when Joni cut him off.

'Because if you don't write it, it won't get written.'

Joni had a way of getting straight to the point.

'You know what we're like.'

She stood there confronting the rest of the class. Everyone, except Pat, nodded. It was incredible how honest they were with each other. And with themselves. They knew they were never going to write it. Bettina shrugged and smiled as if to say, 'That's the way it is.'

I walked a tightrope at Eora. Not everyone was convinced I was there for the right reasons, particularly those outside our tight little group. Apart from the question of appropriation there were other issues, such as being a whitefella in an environment where I represented all that had gone wrong in Indigenous Australia. I had learnt about the labyrinthine nature of black politics and had somehow managed to avoid being caught up in it. But the more success I had with my class the more snide little comments were being made. Writing a show about the Stolen Generations would put me right in the firing line. I just wanted to help with the script and to act as a mentor. I wanted to be the teacher not the writer. Besides, I was busy with other projects and didn't have the time.

A couple of students had found their political voice and were not afraid to give it air. I told them this project was the perfect vehicle for them. Still no volunteers.

'For God's sake!'

Annie had been strangely subdued during these exchanges. She fixed me with one of her trademark glares.

'We can't write it, can we – it's too close to the bone.'

That was it. Of course. If you had been through this horror, writing about it was just too confronting. Someone cracked a joke. It was the Koori way to ironise a tricky situation. I laughed too. They had worn me down.

'Okay. I'll help you write it—'

They were on their feet and into it before I could finish the sentence.

'I said *help*.'

Bettina gave me a pat on the back. She was the mistress of understatement. I don't think the subject of me helping them write 'a few scenes' ever came up again. It was like that. All action and little talk.

We did some improv on the scene when the mother has her baby taken away. Annie was playing the mother. She blew us away. I could see what she meant about it being close to the bone.

They had a writer and we had a title.

Close to the bone

Of course, you know what happened next. Every night I sat down and wrote scenes based on that day's classes, then I'd take them into class the next day to road-test them. I expected lots of feedback. I never got any. No one ever said that a line didn't ring true or that a scene was missing something. As far as writing the bloody thing was concerned, I was flying solo.

We only got half a play written through this process. I tried to hurry them along onto the next part of the story but they loved doing the scenes we'd already written. And they loved watching them; the whole class would be transfixed as each scene was 'played out'. The way they supported each other was incredible. But I needed help in shaping the story.

The scenes I'd written were looking great but that didn't help to get Act 2 written. In the end I wrote Act 2 entirely on my own, which was certainly *not* what I had intended. It wasn't unusual to find yourself doing things at Eora that you wouldn't dream of doing if you were given the option. But if I was writing it there was no way in the world I was going to direct it too. We needed credibility in the community.

I took a deep breath and rang Lydia Miller. I'd met Lydia through the acting world. She'd starred alongside Geoffrey Rush in Belvoir St Theatre's seminal production of *The Diary of a Madman*. I was nervous because of the politically sensitive nature of my involvement as a writer, but she was cool about it. She put together a directorial team of herself, Rhoda Roberts and David Kennedy, and she got Mark Howett on board to do the lighting.

Ringing Lydia was a masterstroke. Not only did she direct it but she designed the set as well. All the key 'creatives' had professional experience. They had industry credibility but, way more importantly, they also had community credibility. They were part of a new generation of Indigenous artists and they were inspirational. Her team lifted the show to heights we'd never thought possible.

There were 11 in the cast and four in the band. Half the cast had never been on stage before. Mark had created a fantastic lighting rig and the result was beautiful. The empty, soulless foyer I'd stumbled into two years earlier was now a theatrical space. The set had been built by the Eora community. Twenty-four people were involved in set and prop construction; another four created the costumes and props. There were two choreographers and two stage managers. The art department created posters, designed programs and took photographs. All in all there were 50 people directly involved in the production and hundreds more indirectly involved.

The opening night in the foyer at Eora was one of those nights where you keep pinching yourself to make sure you're not hallucinating. Everyone was high on adrenalin. I was spinning out – I don't think I have ever been so nervous. Scott took me out for a beer before the show to settle my nerves. I'll never forget us standing there at the bar wondering how the hell we'd got there.

When we walked back into the foyer the place was buzzing. It was packed; the community had come out in force. Backstage the cast were jumping around like they were on hot sand.

The band kicked off. They were loud. Loud and enthusiastic. The audience loved them and they loved the show. I'd never been in an audience like that one. Their support was palpable. They laughed and clapped and hissed and booed and cheered; they cried rivers of tears at the end of the play when Naomi and Rose were reunited. At the curtain call, as they stamped their feet and roared their approval, the cast raised their arms in triumph and I wept tears of pride.

Close to the Bone turned out to be one of those pieces of theatre that develops a life of its own way beyond the dreams of anyone involved in it. It touched audiences in the most extraordinary way. Annie's rationalisation of why I had to write it was reinforced again and again. When I asked a group of elders who sat in the foyer when we took the show to Macksville why they weren't watching it, they too told me it was 'too close to the bone'. They asked me where my mob came from. I explained to them I wasn't a Koori.

'Yes you are,' they said.

I'm not but it was a lovely thing to say.

I watched in awe as the play took off. For the students it was the ride of a lifetime. We played to packed houses at Eora; we took it up the north coast and across to the north-west of New South Wales. It went to the Adelaide Fringe Festival. A professional production was mounted at the Q Theatre in Penrith with four Eora students in leading roles.

Everywhere the show went it received the same heartfelt, passionate response. Some of the cast performed it in the very towns they were stolen from. Some were on their first trip outside Sydney. Some signed autographs for the first time. Everyone got to experience what being a performer was all about. Theory became practice.

Close to the Bone was done from Botswana to Oxford University. It was incredible to think that something that began as a class exercise in Redfern could end up in an end-of-year examination at Oxford. The students had travelled a long way from those first few classes of stamping their feet and saying their names. Some of it was serendipity, but most of it was a result of good educational practice. Education that was inclusive and sensitive to the students' needs. Education that was flexible enough to bend when it needed to. Education that was about the students. Education that wasn't hamstrung by jargon and had real, tangible rewards.

Jeez, I nearly said 'outcomes'!

Teaching at Eora was special because you could get stuck in. You weren't weighed down by endless paperwork and administration. You could do what teachers are supposed to do: teach. There weren't any staff meetings. Well, maybe that's a bit of an exaggeration, but there weren't many. There was definitely no discussion about smoking in toilets or chewing gum under desks. You could wear what you liked; no one looked down their nose at your 'outfit'. No one gave a shit. No one called you 'sir' either.

All the roadblocks to good teaching were removed at Eora. Teachers were valued for what they could offer. It was liberating. No one respected you because you had status or sucked up to you because you'd be marking their work. There weren't any exams or marks in the conventional sense. The audience for that first showing of *Close to the Bone* were the examiners. And they gave the whole class an A+++.

Transitions

Casual challenge

To be a good teacher you need to feel as though you have something to offer. Once the students have stopped listening to you and your message, it's time for someone else to pick up the baton.

That is what happened at Eora. The place changed beyond recognition. TAFE's takeover inevitably led to the kind of administrative demands that I struggle with. I had to teach English as well as drama and writing. I had to mark the roll! And there was now a new breed of students. They were younger and wanted to move on. Whatever else I might have done, I was still a whitefella with a use-by date stamped on my forehead.

I'd been to the top of the mountain with my class when we did *Close to the Bone*. A lot of them went on to get work in film, theatre and television. A couple recorded albums. They charted new waters. But I was like the coach who stays one season too long. I could never replicate what we'd achieved as a group. I'd been there for three incredible years and I failed to see the writing on the wall.

I finished up at Eora directing *Koorabaret*, a revue of sorts, but it wasn't the same. With the new group I hadn't built up the same level of trust that I'd had before, and if you're not trusted as a teacher you're dead in the water. A couple of young guys were suspicious of me; they questioned my motives for being there. Having put so much blood, sweat and tears into the place I didn't feel as though I had anything to prove. At rehearsals there was open hostility if I suggested that people needed to turn up on time. The wheel had turned full circle and I didn't have the energy to start again. It wasn't the teaching that was tough. It was the politics. The anger. The resentment. It was weird because these guys hadn't experienced anywhere near the same degree of personal debasement my former students had endured. It was almost like they assumed the anger on their elders' behalf.

One guy told me I was exploiting Pat. He told Pat I was exploiting him. He told Pat he didn't need me, that he could go out on his own and do his storytelling without our shows. This was nonsense. Pat didn't need me but he did need the support of his Eora family. There was no way he could go out on his own. To put it bluntly, he needed 'the hook' – someone to tell him when to stop. It had worked brilliantly within the framework of our shows. We loved him and respected him. We looked after him without ever patronising him. It was a perfect arrangement.

Pat had been an alcoholic. Eora had not only given him a new lease of life and a new sense of identity, it had saved his life. As the rest of the class moved on to new challenges, this guy tried to convince Pat to do the same. He couldn't, and he didn't. Eora was more than a school: it was a home. Why anyone would encourage Pat to leave never made any sense to me.

Not that *Koorabaret* was a disaster, far from it. And I formed long-lasting working relationships with some of the class who'd begun their time at Eora with *Close to the Bone*. They were into writing and I loved helping them develop their ideas. I didn't have to motivate them. It was when I had to teach acting to people who weren't motivated that I ran out of steam – not to mention directing a show where half the cast was resentful of my involvement.

As I drove home from the last performance of *Koorabaret* I kept glancing in the rear-view mirror. I was scared someone might be following me. It was time to go.

Working at Eora was an incredible privilege but it was also bloody hard work. It was confronting and frustrating on all sorts of levels. It was also as good a teaching experience as you could hope to have.

My next foray into the world of teaching came in the form of casual teaching. Casual teachers fill in for other teachers who are absent. It had been 15 years since I had taught in a secondary school so I had lots of paperwork to do to get state approval. I needed a number.

I'd begun teaching in the New South Wales system and then resigned to go across the border into the ACT system. When I returned to teaching in New South Wales it was in the TAFE system, so there were lots of hoops to jump through before I could get the necessary authorisation. I began to see why teachers were now being referred to as public servants. It wasn't because of their *service* and it certainly had nothing to do with the *public* side of their work. Teachers had become public servants thanks to the mountains of paperwork that now littered every aspect of the profession.

Finally I got my big tick and waited for the phone to ring. At that stage of my life I'd got used to waiting for the phone to ring. The actor's life – staring hopefully at the phone, waiting for that all-important affirmation or audition. Waiting, waiting. But I couldn't wait any more. I had young mouths to feed and financial commitments to meet. I couldn't keep bludging four dollars off my friend every time I wanted to feed my kids sausages on a Friday night.

I was lying in bed happily sleeping off a hangover when the phone rang. I fell out of bed and fumbled around for the receiver.

'Mr Manning?'

Mr Manning? No one called me Mr Manning. It wasn't my agent; I hadn't got another gig on *A Country Practice*. I panicked. Who could be calling at this hour and addressing me like this? The police?

'Yesss …'

'Mr Manning, we have a casual position available for the day. Are you interested?'

'Ohhh, a school?'

'Yes, Mr Manning. A school.'

He named the school. He was getting impatient.

'Are you interested or not?'

Interested? I was stone motherless broke. I'd spent my last tenner on the last shout.

'Of course. Love to.'

'Right. Be here in 20.'

'Where—'

Click.

Twenty? How was I going to get to the other side of the city in peak-hour traffic in 20 minutes? Lear jet?

I chucked on whatever clothes I could lay my hands on. I skipped the shower because time was of the essence. My partner shoved a cup of tea in my hand and an apple in my mouth. I rushed out the door. Balancing the cuppa on one knee and the *Gregory's* on the other, I frantically searched for directions, which had never been my strong suit. Off I spluttered. (I'd like to say 'roared' but I still drove a Kombi.) I turned the corner and the tea landed in my lap. Not only did it scald me but I would be turning up for my first day at school looking like I'd pissed myself. Not a good start to my rebooted school teaching career.

Eventually, having run a dozen red lights, gone down two one-way streets and somehow avoided three head-ons, I arrived at my destination. I swung into the car park and double-parked behind the principal.

I suddenly freaked out. I hadn't been in a school for 15 years.

I rushed across the playground and asked some kids for directions to the deputy's office. They looked at me weirdly. I remembered the wet patch and prayed they wouldn't notice. Thankfully one of them pointed me in the right direction. I felt like Mr Bean.

'You're late.'

'Sorry ...'

I nearly said 'sir' but I remembered I was an adult too. I positioned my bag in an attempt to camouflage my wet crotch but the deputy was way too stressed to notice. His face was red. He had beads of sweat dotting his forehead and great black rings around his eyes. 'Why is he wearing mascara?' I wondered as he handed me my allocation for the day. I didn't ask, of course. I knew not to mess with the deputy. And he was in no mood for small talk. It's incredible how muscle-memory works. After all those years out of schools I immediately slotted back into being a supernumerary. I resumed my place at the bottom of the pecking order.

As I perused my day's allocation I received an unsolicited rant about how difficult it was to find a casual. I learnt that the person I was replacing didn't call to say they were sick until the eleventh hour. The deputy had made 25 calls and finally scraped the bottom of the barrel with me.

My allocation included PGD (playground duty) and PE (or PDHPE, as it was now called). I later discovered that these duties were nearly always included in a casual's allocation. PE teachers seemed to get sick a lot, which was kind of ironic. For many casuals the idea of standing in the middle of a muddy field armed with a footy and a whistle and surrounded by a bunch of testosterone-charged boys was not all that enticing. Particularly if they'd dressed as though they were going to the opera. For me it was heaven on a stick. The rest of my daily allocation was a hotchpotch of 'teaching' the worst classes in the school subjects I'd barely heard of, let alone taught.

In some regards schools had changed dramatically. There was now a far wider range of subjects on offer. There was also a whole raft of new acronyms to learn. No longer were we expected to teach boring old 'subjects'. Now there were KLAs – that's Key Learning Areas. Subjects were organised under the umbrella of KLAs. It was like learning a whole new language. HSIE, for instance: Human Society and Its Environment. Under the HSIE umbrella sat Aboriginal studies, economics, business studies, ancient and modern history, history extension, society and culture (!) and studies in religion.

History was no longer with English, even though English teachers often taught history. English was a stand-alone KLA but poor old history had been lumped in with all the other subjects under the all-encompassing HSIE banner.

Where was my old favourite, woodwork? Woodwork was buried in TAS: Technological and Applied Studies. And even then you couldn't find it. It's in the KLA of Design and Technology. Not sure what happened to manual arts, I think that might have been swallowed by TAS as well. There was even a KLA called Creative Arts. Drama was now a stand-alone subject under the Creative Arts KLA.

PE had become more than just sport. It now encompassed personal development, sex education – although this didn't get its initials in the acronym – health and physical education. Hence the acronym, PDHPE.

The load the deputy handed out crossed subject areas – sorry, KLAs – because the person I was replacing didn't have many classes that day and the deputy wanted to get his money's worth. It was a terrible job organising casuals, particularly on Monday mornings.

It wasn't personal but he took his frustration out on me. He gave me every onerous task he could point a stick at. He hated casuals but we were a necessary evil.

I soon learnt the reason I was there in the first place: the teacher I was replacing was getting counselling to help recover from the classes I'd been allocated. Or had a terrible hangover. Or both.

I was cannon fodder. Again. I wondered how this had happened. Not that long ago I'd starred in a movie that had screened at Cannes and now I was one rung above teenager. At Eora there hadn't been a hierarchy among the teaching staff, but there was one here. It was like I'd never left. It was *Groundhog Day*. It was scary.

While the subject areas had broadened some things hadn't changed at all. The playground had exactly the same energy. It was noisy and bursting with activity. Student year-groups occupied well-marked-out territories. For some there was a range of ball games, for others intense catching up on scandals, for others again, isolation. I loved the playground. It was such a microcosm of teenage life. Adults didn't exist in the playground. You were invisible. You might tell kids to do things or even talk to them, but you weren't part of the action. One thing I'd learnt about kids was that your relationship with them was compartmentalised. In the classroom it was one thing, in the playground it was another, on the sporting field something else, and outside the school something else again.

Another feature that didn't appear to have changed was the architecture. Finding your way around a school was never easy. I eventually found my way through the labyrinth to the staff room. I knocked timidly on the door. No luck. I thought I heard voices inside and thought of knocking again. Finally someone opened the door. They looked me up and down. I looked like some desperado left over from a spaghetti western (an extra, of course). I tried to straighten myself up. I was admitted to the inner sanctum, the staff room.

Now if there had been changes in some aspects of school life, as far as the staff room was concerned, well, the more things change the more they stay the same. The room itself was like every other staff room I'd been in. It was painted regulation grey. The desks faced the wall and were butted up against each other to guarantee an invasion of personal space. There was an old bar-fridge rattling away in the corner, a sink neatly stacked with coffee cups and the world's biggest tin of International Roast, a microwave, a window that hadn't been prised open for half a century, bookshelves cluttered with textbooks, a notice board full of important notices, and lists. Everywhere lists. In the middle of the room there were a few standard-issue blue vinyl 'armchairs' arranged around a Formica table laden with schoolbooks and unopened journals. You couldn't swing a cat in there. A couple of pathetic-looking pot plants and faded posters completed the scene. Our friends the visionary architects from the Soviet Union had been at it again.

A couple of teachers pushed past me as they scurried towards their desks to grab something – anything – for first period. I noticed a couple of old hands sitting at their desks. They didn't acknowledge my existence. I wondered why they hadn't opened the door when I'd knocked 20 minutes earlier. I wondered but I wasn't game to ask. Their body language hardly invited a chinwag. Back in another staff room – and no one knew what the hell I was doing there.

'Who are you?'

'I'm the casual ...'

'Oh right. Away again is he?'

'Can you tell me ...'

'I haven't got time.'

'Ask *X*.' (The head teacher.)

'That's what he/she is paid for.'

'If he/she can get his/her act together.'

'If you can find him/her.'

'He/she is probably crawling to the boss again.'

Pathetic, knowing laughter.

I couldn't believe it. My first play, *Us or Them*, was about this, but I'd written it 15 years ago. Here they all were again: the barely concealed antipathies and jealousies, the tenuous alliances, the ennui, the pockets of equally unbearable enthusiasm, the resignation. I'd portrayed the staff room as a bunker – some were more like a snake pit. All I wanted was to know where A5 was, but it seemed no one would tell me. They were all too busy girding their loins for first period. I must have been a pathetic sight, standing there like a shag on a rock. Fortunately a youngish member of staff took pity on me.

'Hi. I'm Mary.'

'Hi, Mary.'

'He usually leaves some work on his desk.'

'Great.'

'It's over here.'

She led me to what I thought was the rubbish tip but which turned out to be my man's desk. She sifted through the pile of rubble and produced a roll and, thank God, some work.

'How did he know ...'

'He was going to be sick?'

Mary looked at me like I was incredibly naïve, which I still was. What would I know about playing the system? In three years at Tenterfield I took one day off. And I felt guilty about it. I took a couple off at Watson and never missed a class at Eora. It wasn't because I was goody-goody or after a promotion. It just never occurred to me. There was always too much to do.

The bell rang. Mary excused herself and I was caught in the middle of a revolving door as the staff room emptied. What a spectacular fall from grace. At Tenterfield, Watson and Eora I was cock of the walk. Now I was the feather duster. It was back to square one and it was pretty confronting. I tried to ask some kids for directions to A5 but they were too busy to even notice me. As I wasn't part of the furniture, I didn't exist. A casual is just putty, filling in the gaps.

Finally I found my way to A5, which was, helpfully, on the other side of the school and up 25 flights of steps. The kids were waiting but they didn't pay me much attention. I got the impression that they were used to having casuals. I dutifully called the roll but had no idea who anyone was and couldn't pronounce half their names, which immediately put me on the back foot.

'It's *Elena* not Alannah.'

'Sorry. Ramon?'

Four Ramons answered. I was suspicious but let it go through to the keeper. Some of the kids were pointing at me. Was my wet patch still visible?

'Are you on telly?'

Uh oh. I hadn't factored this into the equation. No one at Eora had ever commented on my acting career. Nor had they asked about my personal history, which was probably just as well. They were adults and it didn't mean anything to them. Kids were another matter; their priorities were different and being on telly was a big deal for them. I hadn't taught kids since appearing on TV and I wasn't sure what it would mean. At least the class wasn't rioting. Could I use this newfound, minor celebrity to help me through the day?

'Sometimes.'

'Whatcha been in?'

'Oh, I don't know, lots of things.'

'Are you in that paint ad?'

'Yes.'

That seemed to mollify them. I could have starred in the most cutting-edge piece of television ever made and it wouldn't have mattered. I was in an ad. I had cred.

I decided to let sleeping dogs lie. I didn't want any trouble. I handed out the work that had been left for them and basically spent the rest of the lesson twiddling my thumbs. Nothing much happened. I didn't do any teaching. It was like watching grass grow. Not exactly stimulating.

Back in the relative safety of the trench (the staff room) I inadvertently picked up a coffee cup that belonged to one of the old hands. It was her *favourite* coffee cup. I felt a laser burning into my neck. I turned to face a room full of raised eyebrows. She purposefully walked towards me. I feared castration. She took the cup out of my hand and walked through me to the hot water. Not a word was spoken.

Suitably chastened I sat down at the nearest empty desk. At least I thought it was empty. I looked up to see the owner. She was hovering above me with her cup of herbal tea, poised. Another scalding?

'Sorry, I didn't realise ...'

Some teachers were known to be quite anal. Others territorial. Some anal and territorial, like tomcats. Anal tomcats. The danger for the casual was that you didn't know the ropes. You didn't know the hierarchy. But disturbing the social order around the urn was nothing compared to messing with a teacher's pens. That was tantamount to messing with their heads. Some teachers had all their pens lined up in a special order and woe betide the person who disturbed them. If the kleptomaniac, who may also have been an anarchist, stole a pen from the anal retentive there would be hell to pay. This type of thing would cause simmering resentment. It even might escalate into outright warfare. I too was obsessed with my pens when I started teaching. I think this might have been a sign of insecurity. In later years I could never find one and every pen I put on my desk disappeared.

The kids always knew you were a 'sub'. How they reacted to you had nothing to do with you and everything to do with their relationship with their regular teacher. One of my closest mates was a teacher and, after we had a particularly heavy night on the tiles, he suggested I sub for him. He was as crook as a dog. So was I, but I needed the coin.

'Where's Mr B?

'He's away.'

'Aw no!'

'I'm—'

I was pissing in the wind. They turned their backs on me and caught up on all the latest goss. They didn't even bother opening their bags.

'I've got some work for you ...'

They couldn't have been less interested. They liked Mr B. He was rarely away and they made no attempt to mask their bitter disappointment at the sight of me in his place. It didn't matter how many ads I was in. I wasn't Mr B and that was that. It was nice to see how much my good mate was loved but it didn't help me one bit. I decided to spend another day twiddling my thumbs.

Some people seemed to handle 'child-minding' but I never could. I was too restless; I needed to be doing something. I made the mistake of trying to impart some words of wisdom to a class I was 'looking after'. It happened to be a subject I knew something about. I somehow got their attention and started sharing my infinite knowledge with them. I got about halfway through the second sentence when I realised my words were falling on deaf ears. They were looking at me like I was mad.

'What's he doing?'

'It's a free period.'

'Who does he think he is?'

I gave up and they returned to whatever they were doing.

The worst situation was when their regular teacher was a martinet. The kids filed into class, heads bowed, ready for whatever was going to be dished up to them. Then they saw you – and they saw freedom. Celebrations broke out. Bags flew through the air. They danced, hugged, gave each other high fives. It was like being in the city square when a dictator is deposed.

Trying to settle the revellers down was a major challenge. You had to get in quick – if you waited too long you had no chance. You had to bring out the big guns and assume control. You drew upon all the skills you had developed in quelling riots.

Experienced teachers had an uncanny ability to do this. Whether it was body language or the way they addressed the class or some other indefinable quality, I don't know. I do know that it had nothing to do with the sex or the size of the teacher. It certainly wasn't about physical intimidation. After a few years of teaching most teachers just demanded respect. And they got it.

Somehow, somewhere along the line I picked up a few of these tricks of the trade. I never thought about it or analysed it. It was instinctive. I never resorted to the uniquely physical approach of my manual arts adversary back at Tenterfield. I never raised my voice or got angry. I just waited for calm to be restored.

In this regard, experience was definitely the best teacher, especially when you picked up work as a casual. I was lucky, I had experience; but for others who were starting a teaching career as a casual, it was way more problematic. A friend of mine, who happened to be a highly regarded performer, got his first taste of teaching as a casual. George might have been one of the country's most persuasive actors but he could *never* get a key out of the head teacher. He would dutifully find his way to the designated classroom and discover the door was locked – and the kids getting increasingly restless.

'Wait here, guys. I'll get a key.'

'Hey, aren't you George from *Play School*?

He'd race back to the staff room to find the head teacher. No luck. And of course as a casual he didn't have a key to the staff room either. Being the resourceful type, George would eventually track Mr Purvis down.

'Excuse me, I need a key …'

Mr Purvis would roll his eyes.

'I'll open it for you.'

As if he were perversely underlining the point that George was a casual and didn't know the ropes, Mr Purvis would traipse all the way across the playground to open the door for him. Did he think George was going to do a runner with the keys? Or did he want to put him in his place? The absurdity of this was that George was highly skilled and could have offered the kids a lot if he'd been given some encouragement. This often happened with casuals. They were categorised as 'hopeless' or 'lazy'. Maybe some of the regular teachers were worried the casuals might show them up? In most other environments a substitute would be welcomed; the bench player offering fresh legs to lift the team.

Of course there were plenty of upsides to casual teaching – apart from the money, which was pretty good and certainly more than you'd get if you stayed in bed. It gave you a chance to get a bird's eye view of how a particular school worked. And because everyone essentially ignored you, it gave you a chance to observe teachers at work. In my case it served to reinforce the respect I already had for the profession, no matter how eccentric some teachers might be. Nevertheless, to survive as a casual teacher you need a thick skin, a sense of humour and a low-boredom threshold. And the capacity to play very low status.

The most extraordinary experience I had as a casual teacher was at Rivendell in Sydney's Concord West. Rivendell was a school for kids with personality disorders and behavioural problems. It had a teaching staff as well as doctors and nurses. Its tranquil setting on the banks of the Parramatta River provided a welcome antidote to the tumultuous lives of the kids who attended it. It had a collection of magnificent old sandstone and brick buildings, lots of space and beautiful gardens. It had once been a convalescence hospital. Henry Lawson took some 'time out' there. Its name comes from Tolkien's *The Hobbit* – Rivendell was a safe haven for the Hobbits, a place to recharge the batteries. It was the perfect environment for a school.

I thought I'd dealt with some difficult teaching assignments before I worked at Rivendell. I hadn't scratched the surface. But what struck me about the people who worked at Rivendell, aside from their obvious commitment, was their sense of humour. They had a capacity to deflect difficult situations with humour.

The principal was gay, and when a kid called him a 'bloody poofter' he told him it was inappropriate to swear. He was fantastic.

A kid once said to the deputy, 'Fuck you and fuck your mother.'

'That's not very nice,' the deputy replied. 'I'm very fond of my mother.'

I'm told the kid turned 'Fuck you and fuck your mother' into a rap song.

The truth was I didn't have the qualities to teach at a school like Rivendell. I didn't have the patience and I didn't have the intestinal fortitude to withstand the constant barrage of abuse you might be subjected to. Nor was I emotionally strong enough to deal with the kind of problems these kids had encountered – to look them in the face knowing what they had been through.

It's one of the hardest things about teaching. You find out that a kid has been abused in some way and then you remember how you gave them a hard time over something relatively insignificant. It makes you feel like shit. For example, I once had a confrontation with a student over a lie. I had incontrovertible proof that she had lied and I tried to break her down, to get her to admit it. I interviewed – or should I say interrogated? – her with a couple of senior members of staff. We never broke her. She stuck to her guns. I later discovered her drunken father had made her stand on a table while he looked up her dress to check her virginity. It made me sick.

I could hardly look her in the face after I made that discovery but I had to carry on as though everything was normal. She never knew that I, or anyone else, was aware of her shocking ordeal. No wonder she struggled with the truth. We got on quite well, even after the interrogation. To her it was water off a duck's back. She'd told a lie – she knew it and I knew it – but what did it matter in the context of her life? I could only wonder at the emotional cost for people who dealt with this kind of thing every day. I don't know how those teachers did it.

After working at Rivendell I took some casual work at a leading selective girls high school. It was about as far away from Rivendell as you could imagine, and even further from Tenterfield. The girls were all highly intelligent and regarded me with barely disguised contempt. They too loved their regular teacher; I was only there to fill the space left behind. Talk about feeling useless. I handed out their work. They did it. That was that. I'd look out the window and count down the seconds.

By now I'd realised that I couldn't survive casual teaching. I'd die of boredom. But then I was handed a lifeline: the drama teacher at the selective school told me I should apply for drama marking. I didn't know what she was talking about.

Practical marking

I discovered that drama had not only become a subject in its own right but that kids could now take it for the HSC. It was composed of 40 per cent theory and 60 per cent practice. In spite of this, the department didn't recognise drama as a 'practical' subject. It still doesn't – art is practical, as are music and dance, but not drama. This has something to do with staffing and class sizes, as 'practical' subjects have a limit to how many kids can be in a class. Consequently there is no limit to the size of a drama class.

Despite not being recognised as a 'practical' subject there was still a need, contradictory as it seems, for practical performances in drama to be marked. Every kid who took it at HSC had to do an individual performance and a group performance. The group performance was compulsory. It involved between three and six students creating an 8 to 12-minute piece of theatre. It had to be completely self-devised and was incredibly demanding.

On the day of the HSC these practical performances were marked by a team of two, sometimes three markers. The individual performance was a 6 to 8-minute routine drawn from any piece of theatre writing or devised by the students themselves. Even though the individual performance was more demanding than the group performance, the vast majority of students chose it over the design or written tasks.

Consequently practical marking was a huge operation, with pairs of markers being sent all over the state to mark these performances. They went to the most remote rural communities as well as to every nook and cranny in the cities. It involved spending a fortnight out of school, so it was sometimes difficult to get principals to agree to let their teachers go. This meant that someone like me, who wasn't attached to a school, had a good chance of getting the job. I was pretty broke at the time so I decided to apply and, to my surprise, I got the gig. The boss of marking was an old mate from university, which might have had something to do with my appointment, although Mel swears no nepotism was involved.

I turned up at the school where they were holding the pilot marking. It was called Newtown High School of the Performing Arts, a specially designated performing arts high school. I'd never heard of it. It was relatively new: it had been formed by the amalgamation of two 'normal' high schools and had only been going for a couple of years. It had its own theatre and was in a great location. Mel was the head of English and drama there.

The pilot marking was held to set marking standards and it took place over three days, including a weekend. I went along ignorant but intrigued. How were they going to mark acting? Having worked in professional theatre and been on the receiving end of good and bad reviews I was sceptical of objectivity when it came to assessing performance. Surely only subjectivity could account for such a disparity of opinion among critics?

I was immediately struck by the incredible enthusiasm of the teachers chosen to do the marking. It was like their hands had been untied and they were suddenly free to do what they loved. They had fought to get their principal's support and now they were going to prove it was worth it. They owned their subject and were determined to find the fairest way to assess the kids' performances. I had never been involved in anything like this.

Drama was still a relatively small subject at that stage, with something like 1000 candidates and 20 markers. Today there are about 6000 kids doing drama and around 50 markers in New South Wales alone. In Victoria it's about 4000. Drama might have been the fastest growing subject in the country but in 90 per cent of schools it had to fight to be accepted; these drama teachers had been prepared to do 'whatever it took' to do just that.

Mel was a remarkable woman. She'd been one of the teachers who fought for drama's inclusion as an HSC subject and for the inclusion of the practical performance. Mel was one of those extraordinary people who could be totally in control and exude calm and sensitivity at the same time. She argued for a proper debrief after the kids had performed; only someone who'd been on stage could understand how important that was. The debrief involved the markers asking each candidate a number of set questions. It wasn't part of the assessment process, although it could bring to light any plagiarism or 'coaching', which was illegal. Its primary purpose was to give the kids a chance to wind down, to let off steam and share their pride. It was an example of teaching at its best because it put the needs of the kids front and centre. It was a brilliant thing to do.

My fears about not being able to assess performance were allayed. Mel and her team had devised a system whereby you marked kids according to a set list of criteria, such as if their voice was clear, whether their movement was motivated, and if what they were saying and doing was believable. You basically ticked off each skill as you watched the performance. It took subjectivity out of the equation. Your job wasn't to assess whether you liked the piece or not; your personal opinion or prejudices were irrelevant. You were never marking *what* a candidate was saying but *how* they were saying it. It was all about skills.

Some students from Newtown were used as guinea pigs for

the pilot marking. They devised and performed group pieces that we marked, like a 'dummy' HSC. We sat alone for the marking. When the performance was over, the students left; once they were out of earshot, Mel chose someone at random to read out their marks. It was nerve-wracking. If your marks were way off there was nowhere to hide. For instance, if the bulk of the markers gave a particular kid between 25 and 28 out of 30 and you gave them 10 it was obvious you were out of kilter. You had to look at yourself and question what you were missing. Not surprisingly it was usually a result of subjectivity creeping in; if you hated the content of a piece, you would tend to mark it down. But of course there was no place on the mark sheet for your opinion. Your job was to give marks for the skills on display. And, most importantly, your job was to reward, not penalise.

It was demanding and challenging. It required enormous concentration to watch six kids perform and to give all of them an individual mark. You had to separate each one. You had to follow the piece *and* focus on the skills being demonstrated. You had to cover all bases: voice, movement, character, cohesion of the piece. If you blinked you missed something. You could neither ease into it nor sit back and enjoy it. And it wasn't like auditioning where you can dismiss someone after their first few lines. You had to look to reward them no matter what. And the stakes couldn't be higher – it was the HSC after all. To my surprise my marks weren't discrepant; I was on track with everyone else. What a relief.

Marking was not a bludge. The teachers at pilot marking gave up their weekend to put themselves through the wringer so they could get the fairest possible result for the kids. It was what dedicated teachers did, and for no kudos or reward except the knowledge that the kids would be given every opportunity to shine. They did it because they were professionals and because they loved their subject. The whole process was irresistible and inspiring. It seduced me.

There were a few intense moments when it came to discussion of marks. One group of girls did a piece about 'westies'. They were all blonde and conventionally pretty; I think they might have been dancers. The piece was patronising and condescending towards people who were less fortunate than they were. It might have been called sexist and borderline racist. It was definitely controversial.

The bulk of the markers were women, just like the bulk of drama students are girls. And when these highly intelligent, politicised women saw this piece of sexist, bigoted theatre, their collective hackles rose. If they had been in a theatre they might have walked out or even thrown their shoes at the performers. But they weren't in a theatre, they were in a pilot examination.

Some of them gave the girls really low marks. I leapt to my feet and defended them. I wasn't defending the content of the piece, I was defending their skill level. I argued that a group could do a piece championing Nazism and still get high marks. (Years later I was in a school where three boys did a piece about rape that was extremely disturbing. They were scary. In terms of 'belief' their skill-levels were high, so they got rewarded in that category. But their overall skill-levels were poor and they finished well under the required time limit, which showed up how superficial their piece was. Thankfully they got the marks they deserved.) These girls weren't brilliant but they weren't terrible either. Once I'd finished my defence of them one of the markers, a gun teacher from Newtown, shot me down in flames. She had been suspicious of me from the start. Just because I was an actor and a writer, who did I think I was? She was pretty forthright. I gave as good as I got and the girls ended up with the mid-range marks they deserved. Of course, I was to become good friends with my newly acquainted foe.

For some reason teachers will often have an unhealthy attitude towards professionals who practise in their field. Drama teachers can be overly critical of shows and art teachers can unfairly bag exhibitions. Maybe this is because teachers aren't treated like true professionals themselves. They work their guts out and still they are constantly categorised as bludgers. If teachers were afforded the status they deserve, they might be more willing to embrace other professionals. The system itself makes cross-fertilisation very difficult; education departments and teachers' unions both put up far too many bureaucratic hurdles to allow the kind of sharing of skills that would benefit the whole of society.

Pilot marking was an eye-opener. If you doubted the professionalism of teachers, you would have changed your mind after that weekend.

Mel asked if I'd be interested in any work at Newtown if it happened to come up. After that introduction, how could I resist? In that little theatre there were teachers who would cut off their right arm for their kids. Their dedication was infectious and it snapped me out of my complacency. That's the thing about good teaching – its passion is irresistible.

When it was time for marking we were paired up and sent out on the road. In those days the first week was in the country and the second in the city. I loved it. I loved travelling from town to town and school to school. We stayed in dodgy hotels, met up for even dodgier dinners and shared our experiences of life on the road marking. In those early years we were a small band, members of a pretty tight club. The work was demanding but Mel had set a tone that made everyone want to rise to the challenge. We were like travelling salesmen, selling the joys of HSC drama around the state.

It was gruelling but no one complained. We had to travel great distances and the hours were long. Arriving at 8.30 am sometimes involved a very early start to get to the town and then the school we were marking in. And we had to factor in getting lost. The city leg was a nightmare in this regard. There was traffic to consider and, in my case, my ineptitude with a map. Then there was parking. I much preferred the country leg.

Once we found our school we'd mark however many groups and individual performances were on show then hop in the car and head off to the next location, which might be 150 kilometres away. It wasn't a gig for the faint-hearted. I have an enduring image of one of the markers hurrying across the road, red overcoat trailing behind her like Superwoman, arms laden with marking sheets, glasses perched precariously on the end of her nose, trying desperately to figure out if she was at the right school. That's the way it was for most of us.

After we'd marked at the last school for the day, we'd sit down and collate all the marks. This would take hours as we argued over marks and ranks. Mostly we'd agree but there were inevitably disagreements that needed to be ironed out. The whole thing took incredible organisational skills to bring together and the department deserves credit for this.

Indeed, one school I marked at, way out the back of beyond, had three kids doing HSC drama; we had one group and two individuals to mark. We drove over 200 kilometres to get there and after barely an hour we were off again. I thought it sent a pretty good signal that the department would send a couple of examiners all that way for an hour's marking. The whole school was abuzz when we got there. The principal greeted us as if we had crossed the desert on a camel train.

'Mr Burke and Ms Wills?'

His hospitality was boundless. The Iced Vo Vos were on tap. Kids hung out windows waving as the principal escorted us across the playground.

'Give 'em a good mark!'

'They're really good!'

They had a public showing the night before and half the town had turned up. A queue had already formed to offer support. We had to point out that there was a limit to audience numbers and that Year 12 students and parents couldn't watch. It was after all an HSC examination, although it seemed to have taken on a far greater significance.

We were greeted by the teacher in charge who looked as though she was going to vomit or pass out, or both. She looked about 12. I wanted to give her a hug but that might have sent the wrong signal. I have never seen anyone so nervous – 'cat on a hot tin roof' doesn't begin to describe it.

'I've never taught drama before.'

There were obviously all sorts of protocols to observe to keep the whole thing above board. Chatting about the kids we were about to assess was definitely not one of them.

'We have bit of paperwork to go through.'

'The kids love it.'

'Just a few standard questions.'

'How could I say no?'

'Um, if we could—'

'It's been so good for them.'

'Uh huh ...'

'I can't tell you what I've been through.'

No. You can't.

We managed to get the paperwork done and made our way into the room set aside for the examination. It was a 'portable', a temporary classroom, and pretty flimsy.

'We couldn't get the hall. PE.'

Some people, like me, still called it PE.

'Is it okay if I watch?'

'Of course it is. You're the class teacher.'

I so wanted to wish her luck.

Of course, there was no theatre at this school – it was a state school. Desks and chairs had been cleared to make a playing space. It was pretty basic. This was why the emphasis on marking skills and nothing else was so crucial. It had to be a level playing field – kids at a wealthy private school with their own theatre, lighting rigs and high-tech sound systems couldn't be advantaged over kids without such resources. As markers we had to ignore the surrounds and focus solely on the skills on display. No amount of money or cajoling could buy our marks!

The whittled-down audience grinned at us as we took our seats at the marking table. They were on their very best behaviour and willing us to give their mates good marks. I started shivering. A cold wind blew through a broken window and the one-bar heater was proving ineffective. My teeth started chattering. I sat on my hands and then remembered I'd need one of them for marking. I nodded to the teacher. She gave the thumbs-up to the Year 9 kid who was operating the tinny portable sound system.

We sat there waiting. And waiting.

'Oh shit. I forgot ... how silly of me.'

The teacher rushed off. She'd forgotten to tell the kids they were on. Red-faced, she came rushing back in followed by her kids. And they were *her* kids. I looked at them and wondered what she had gone through to get them there. They lined up. They looked like rabbits caught in a spotlight.

'We just need to check your numbers.'

The line-up was about identifying each kid and matching them with their examination number. It didn't take long with just three. The first in line was a boy who looked like he lived exclusively on a diet of Maccas. Next to him a little girl who looked as though she had got out of primary school for the day. The last boy was so shy he could hardly say his number.

'Try and relax.'

'We're just checking your numbers.'

'When you're ready.'

And away they went. If truth be told there was little chance the Sydney Theatre Company would be offering them a contract. Their eight minutes seemed like eight hours. But – and it's a big BUT – that wasn't the point. They were totally into what they were doing. They were loving it. They were trying their guts out. In terms of commitment they made some of the seasoned professionals I'd seen going through the motions look like amateurs. They were there doing the HSC and they were having the time of their lives. I wished I'd enjoyed my HSC as much as these guys did. They were on cloud nine.

We marked their skills. We focused on their voices and their movement and their characters. Whether the piece itself represented the latest in cutting-edge theatre practice was irrelevant.

They couldn't shut up during the debrief. Even the boy who couldn't talk piped up.

'Whatcha think?'

We couldn't say.

'We spent hours and hours rehearsin'.'

'Yeah, we went over to Troy's at the weekend.'

I guessed there had been a bit of a party at Troy's, even though they weren't meant to tell us their names.

'I don't mind this acting stuff.'

'Yeah, its pretty cool, eh?'

'I was pretty scared but.'

'Yeah!'

'Nearly pissed meself.'

They laughed. We tried to put the genie back in the bottle but there was no corking these guys. They more than answered our questions. When the debrief was over they exploded out of the room and into their teacher's arms. She was bursting with pride. It was like they had all won the lottery. They hooped and hollered and it was one of the most fantastic things I'd ever seen.

I was hooked. If I needed any prompting to go back into the classroom I got it then and there. I wanted to be part of this.

Marking drama made a lot of the work I'd done as an actor seem a bit self-indulgent and rather pointless. This had a point. It was about kids getting up on their feet and expressing themselves. Kids who weren't necessarily natural performers. Kids who were shy and lacked confidence. Kids who grew ten-feet-tall when they overcame their fears.

That's not to say it was all peaches and cream. Some pieces dragged. There was a sameness about some of them that was soporific and I needed to prop open my eyelids on more than one occasion, but even then I reminded myself what I was doing, of where my responsibilities lay. I know for a fact that doing HSC drama changed some kids' lives forever. It opened their eyes to possibilities they had never dreamt of. That was pretty cool.

When Mel offered me the chance to be part of the action, to do a six-week block at Newtown, how could I refuse?

Teaching Heaven

Double drama

I told myself I had no intention of returning to full-time teaching, so a block of work was very appealing both in financial terms and because I didn't want to give up acting and writing. Teaching a six-week block also meant that I was more than just a babysitter; unlike day-to-day casual teaching I could really get my teeth into it. It was perfect.

The first thing I noticed as I walked across the playground was that the Australian Aboriginal flag was flying. How far we'd travelled since I first went teaching. The flag was designed in 1971, two years before I was sent to Tenterfield. Now, 20 years later, I was back but in a very different sort of high school.

The pilot marking experience hadn't given me any indication of what Newtown High School of the Performing Arts, in inner-city Sydney, was really like. We'd been locked inside and, because pilot marking was held over a weekend, there weren't any kids around. The fact that the school had its own theatre did set it apart from most schools I'd come across. There was an amphitheatre in the middle of the playground: a homage to the foundation of Western theatre in Ancient Greece? It was painted with an Indigenous motif.

I was immediately knocked out by the energy in the place. There were kids doing all the usual things that kids do in a playground but there was something else too. As well as ball games and typical high-octane teenage behaviour, there were kids doing things I'd never seen in a playground: some were practising dance steps, twirling on their toes, pirouetting, doing pointe work and the splits, others were performing cartwheels, juggling, walking on their hands. It was a cross between the Australian Ballet and Circus Oz. Then there were bunches of kids sitting around playing guitars and nodding their heads like young guitar heroes. I heard music coming out of a building and looked up to see a girl in the window belting out something operatic. At another window a boy was blowing away on a trumpet. It was a long way from wild cats being set loose in the playground. This was something else entirely.

The drama department was in a 100-year-old building that had once been home to Newtown Primary School. Walking up the stone stairs and into the building was like walking into a cathedral. The first things that struck me were the high ceilings and the detailed fretwork. It was one of those buildings where you could smell the history. I could have been in Europe. It was certainly a far cry from a standard-issue government school. I climbed the carefully preserved staircase and came across a group of kids in earnest discussion.

'Hi.'

They were too busy dissecting the latest play they'd seen – and hated, of course – to engage in small talk.

'Can you tell me where the drama staff room is?'

They pointed.

'Thanks.'

In the corridor I could hear voices in a classroom. I opened the door to find it was a dance studio, with mirrors and barres along the walls. There were some kids inside rehearsing.

'Oh. Sorry.'

They didn't miss a beat and kept on rehearsing. I quietly closed the door and made my way down the carpeted hall towards the staff room.

'Stell-a! Stell-a!'

I wasn't game to open *that* door. What kind of a hole had I tumbled down? The bell hadn't gone and there were kids everywhere, working, rehearsing; and there didn't appear to be a teacher in sight. A couple of kids were waiting outside the staff room.

'Can you give this to Miss Rutherford?'

Even the teachers had theatrical sounding names.

'You're an actor.'

Ahh. Recognition.

'Well, yes ...'

I waited for them to ask what I'd been in. They handed me their books, turned on their heels and strode off. What was the big deal? I was an actor. Like their music teachers were musicians.

There was a noise like a tornado roaring up the stairs. It was Vanessa, my adversary from marking. She flew past me and into the staff room.

'Vanessa?'

I was left in her wake. The kids who had ignored me turned and raced after her into the staff room. One of them metaphorically fell to her knees.

'Sorry I missed rehearsals. I—'

'I don't care what you did. We couldn't do Scene 4. We're behind. We haven't got time.'

'But—'

'There are no buts. You're either dedicated or you're not.'

'I'm dedicated.'

'When are you going to show me?'

'I'm sorry, Hendo.'

All the kids called Vanessa Hendo.

'I'm busy.'

She slammed the door. The kids were shattered. They walked off talking in whispered tones. I got the feeling they wouldn't miss another rehearsal. I also got the feeling that I should wait till Vanessa calmed down. Then I remembered I was a teacher, not to mention a fellow adult, and knocked on the door.

'Come in!'

I walked in carrying the kids' books.

'Hi!'

She was busy rifling through her desk.

'We met at marking.'

Why did I say that? Why did I remind her that I was the smart-arse who thought he knew it all? She looked at me.

'You're taking Jonno's classes?'

Was it a question or was she challenging me?

'Yes.'

At the mention of Jonno's name everyone's ears seemed to prick up. They all said hello, which was a vast improvement on my other casual teaching experiences. The staff room was jam-packed. There were three dance teachers and four drama teachers cheek by jowl. As far as teachers' conditions were concerned, it was a normal school after all. I was shown to a desk and given my allocation.

No time for small talk. Vanessa filled me in and showed me where each of my classes were up to. Being fourth term, the school was pumping more than usual, which was saying something. As well as day-to-day teaching, there were practical and theoretical assessments coming up: performances and essays. There were company and ensemble performances, which came under the umbrella of showcase concerts. These were open to the public and a small stipend was charged. In those days companies were selected by audition and ensembles were classwork. On top of these was a range of end-of-year activities, including the HSC, performing in things like the school spectacular, state drama company productions, the 'Prom' and, finally, presentation day. It was going to be a busy six weeks. I had classes in all years from 7 to 11. Year 12 were doing their HSC.

Mel was in charge of both drama and English so I didn't see a lot of her; she was in another building across the playground. Drama shared a building with art and dance. St George's Hall, a grand Victorian Italianate building, was being restored to house dance the following year. Brand new studios were being built and the magnificent interior restored to its former glory. Music was next door in another old part of the school. The performing arts weren't struggling for air like they were in other schools, they were what the joint was all about.

No one seemed to walk to class, or anywhere else for that matter; it was full steam ahead the whole time. I didn't have time to draw breath before I was heading down the corridor for my first real class with teenagers in 16 years. I didn't know what to expect. Until recently I didn't know that drama was even a subject in schools and that there was such a thing as a performing arts high school. Now I was in one and about to teach Year 11.

I opened the door to Drama One. Another studio. No chairs, no desks, no blackboard, no wood-fired heater in the corner. The kids weren't lounging about affecting cool. They were sitting up straight, in a circle, eagerly waiting to get into it. Frankly, it was a bit unnerving.

'I'm Ned ...'

For a moment I forgot I was back teaching in a high school. At Eora if the students called me anything it was usually Ned. Casual teachers didn't have names so I didn't get called anything when I'd filled in at the other schools. Then I remembered where I was, and who I was.

'Errr ... Mr Manning.'

'Hi.'

'You're replacing Jonno?'

'Um, yeah. I'll be taking you for the next few weeks, until the end of the year.'

'Can we get on with our rehearsals?'

'We've got an assessment.'

'Sure …'

That was it. They were on their feet and into their groups.

'If you need any …'

Vanessa had told me they were rehearsing for an assessment. I didn't realise this meant they would get stuck into it without any input from me. The kids were doing what they loved and didn't need a lot of encouragement to do it. That was the ethos of the place.

That first day was a whirlwind. All my classes were busy rehearsing for assessments so all I had to do was keep up, which took some doing. A few groups showed me what they were working on and I gave them feedback. I felt useful, as though I was contributing something, not just filling in time or engaging in crowd control.

As well as my teaching load I was given Jonno's company. This meant rehearsals after school and on weekends. This didn't phase me; after all, I'd been working in a profession where there isn't any such thing as overtime. You work for as long as it takes. And then some. It was like that at Eora too.

My new company was doing *Lysistrata* by Aristophanes. I knew the play and thought it an odd choice. It was a satire about how Greek and Spartan women in the 5th century BC banded together and withheld sexual favours from their men until they agreed to stop fighting each other. It sure was a long way from *Jabberwocky* in the park at Tenterfield or *My Fair Lady* at Watson. I was assured that the kids were mature enough to handle it. Schools had certainly changed. I was thought a radical for doing *The Removalists*, but compared to *Lysistrata* it's like a pantomime. I wasn't all that comfortable rehearsing a play that was sexually explicit with teenagers and some of the girls were strangely antagonistic towards me. It was rumoured that Jonno had somehow crossed the line as far as teacher–student relationships were concerned. I don't know if that was true or not and I wasn't interested in finding out. All I wanted to do was rehearse.

It immediately struck me that being middle-aged made teaching a different ball game. Not only did I seem to have acquired some authority, but I was so distant in age from the kids that they had no interest in me personally. They didn't bother testing me out like the kids had at Tenterfield. When I was a 22-year-old I was fair game; now I was in my forties I was over the hill. In many ways this made teaching easier. There were no hidden agendas on either side. I didn't feel as though I had to prove myself, and they couldn't have cared less about me. All they cared about was what I had to teach.

It was incredibly liberating to be able to focus solely on the material. There was too much to do to spend time mucking around; there was no chit-chat, no time for gossip, no time for anything other than the job at hand.

I had very little cred when I started at Newtown. Apart from Mel, who knew me, and the principal who liked the fact that I still worked in 'the business', the rest of the staff couldn't have been less impressed with my biography. Just because I was an actor didn't mean I would be a good teacher, which was true, although I was a teacher before I was an actor. Nor did it mean that I would necessarily be a good director.

The principal at Newtown was a one-off. Now I think about it, I never referred to *her* as the boss. She was more like the AD, the artistic director. Once, when she rang to tell me the show I'd directed, an interpretation of *Waltzing Matilda* by Year 7s, was below my 'usual standard', I told her, 'Fair enough, Joan. You're the AD.' I was being ironic but she didn't bat an eyelid. As far as she was concerned she *was* the AD.

She didn't walk around the school, she swept around it. She would lob into classes without warning, break into a soft-shoe shuffle at the drop of a hat, and castigate the girls for not wearing 'shoes with a closed toe', whatever that meant. She doted on the school like it was her baby, which in many ways it was: she had been a driving force behind its conception, its gestation, its birth, its baby steps, its early childhood and its ultimate maturation.

She saw every performance at the school, whether it was dance, drama or music, no matter what the year level, and she had notes to give on every one of them. She tried to keep up with current trends in the professional world by attending as many live performances as possible. I often saw her in theatre foyers around town. She would bowl up to me and I'd introduce her to whomever I was talking to. She loved meeting actors and writers and directors and she loved the theatre world. She was determined to make Newtown one of the best performing arts high schools in Australia, if not the world. In fact, she often boasted it *was* the best in the world. Newtown was very good at talking itself up.

She was a force of nature and she was not against bending the rules if it meant getting things done. She made it possible for me to keep working in the industry while teaching at the school. In this regard she was quite a visionary, not because she recognised my particular talents but because she wanted artists in the school.

Many artists would love to work in education but they can't because they would have to give up performing. In Australia, unlike the rest of the world, there is a silly demarcation line that forces artists to choose between the two. It's a compromise they should never have to make. The school system should welcome people who have so much to offer. It should be able to accommodate professionals from other disciplines who don't have teaching degrees but have a lifetime of experience to offer students. Joan recognised this and she worked wonders to make it possible for me to keep writing and acting while I taught at the school. She could see the big picture. Not surprisingly, the department wasn't quite sure how to deal with her.

My version of *Lysistrata* barely passed muster. Vanessa produced a version of Louis Nowra's *The Golden Age* that remains one of the most incredible things I've ever seen performed by kids. In fact, *the* most incredible. She raised the bar way above my head. The production values for her shows at Newtown were unbelievable. She drove the kids really hard and they loved her for it. When doing a show she was a dynamo, like a woman possessed. She invented the 'Newtown Ha!', a fantastic warm-up exercise that taught focus to Year 7 kids. She was an expert on Meyerhold and Boal, two of the most influential theatre practitioners of the 20th century; their work challenged the orthodoxy of the day. I'd barely heard of them. No wonder she thought I was a bit of an imposter.

Vanessa and Mel were a great, if sometimes tempestuous, combination. They were both visionaries in their own way and they both fought with Joan. These three women were complex, driven individuals and together they lifted drama at Newtown to great heights. As an outsider all I could do was watch in awe. At that time, as far as drama was concerned, it was Newtown first and daylight second – no other school in the state came close. For someone like me who'd been out of teaching for so long, it was extraordinary to witness these advances. It was as if I'd been teaching drama in the Dark Ages. My eyes were opened to a whole new world of possibilities.

One of the more eccentric teachers on the staff, Groucho, was strangely obsessed with *The Insect Play*. It was written by Josef and Karel Capek and explores a metaphorical world of horny butterflies, avaricious dung beetles and argumentative ants. Groucho must have performed every possible reading of *The Insect Play* – he even turned it into a musical. Groucho was a one-off. He made me look like a boring old fart. The kids loved him.

Year 11 moved on to *commedia dell'arte*. I didn't know the first thing about it. Vanessa pointed me in the right direction and I sat up all night taking notes and preparing lessons. I approached teaching *commedia* with a fair amount of confidence – totally misplaced, of course. In fact, I approached the whole gig at Newtown with confidence. That's what time in the classroom gives you. It's probably what surviving Tenterfield gave me. My knowledge might have been limited but these kids were pushovers compared to those I'd cut my teeth with. Besides, I was an actor, I'd faked it before.

I walked into Year 11 carrying a box of *commedia* masks, the notes I'd been up all night preparing and a textbook. I needed the notes and the textbook because I didn't know what the hell I was doing. Year 11 was already there, of course, sitting in a circle.

'Where have you been?'

'You're late.'

'Sorr-y.'

A girl called Helga looked at me with her arms folded, as if to say, 'Who do you think you are? I've seen you act. You're shit.'

Helga questioned everything I said, even the things I knew something about. She was able to smell a rat a mile off and she'd already sussed out that I was fumbling around in the dark with *commedia*. More worrying was that while Helga questioned every word I said, others were hanging onto them for dear life. There was a girl in class who looked like Grace Kelly and lapped up every word I uttered. It freaked me out; I didn't deserve that kind of respect.

I started with some theory: the history of *commedia*, its place in the theatrical landscape, how it had influenced everyone from

Shakespeare to Chaplin. I explained that a lot of clowning sprang from *commedia*. It was going well. I extrapolated from my notes. Even Helga seemed vaguely satisfied. But teaching *commedia* wasn't just about theory; it was also about practice. These kids patiently absorbed the theory but what they really wanted was to get their teeth into the practical stuff. They wanted to get on their feet.

Commedia characters were defined by their masks or, in the case of the lovers, their costumes. So the first step was to recognise the masks and what type of characters they represented. This was easy: I held up the masks and read out the finer points that defined each character. But *commedia* also involved a range of very particular movements associated with each character. The audience knew who was who by the mask they wore and the way they moved. When I started reading from my notes about characters strutting around or continually bumping into things and falling over, Helga piped up.

'Why don't you show us?'

'I'm not an expert ...'

'You're an actor, aren't you?'

'Yes, but ...' There was nowhere to hide. 'Okay. I'll give it a shot.'

I'd told them to be brave, to take risks, now I had to lead by example. I grabbed Arlecchino's mask and started trying to demonstrate how one of *commedia*'s most popular characters moved. Arlecchino was really athletic and really stupid. He'd look everywhere for his donkey and discover he was sitting on it. He'd accidentally drop a letter and do an amazing somersault to retrieve it. Then he'd eat it.

I lowered my centre of gravity, thrust my pelvis forward and, pointing my toes outwards, started moving around. Someone handed me a letter. I pretended to drop it. Then I did a somersault, picked it up and stuffed it in my mouth. The adrenalin coursing through my veins enabled me to pretend I was 20 years younger. I was hoping to relieve the kids of any pressure by making a complete idiot of myself. Although, at that stage, I didn't know quite how much of an idiot.

Not only was Arlecchino a ratbag he was also lascivious. He had an eye for the ladies but he was anything but classy. For some reason I decided to show them a classic scenario where Arlecchino suddenly spies a beautiful woman. I was full of bravado – maybe some Arlecchino had rubbed off on me. So when the imaginary pretty girl walked by, I did what any self-respecting clown would have done to share his lust with the audience. I grabbed my crotch.

Yep.

Frozen in front of a Year 11 class wearing a *commedia* mask with my hand on my crotch, I came to my senses. I realised what I was doing. I'm glad Joan didn't walk in because even she might have drawn the line at that. I quickly removed my hand and slowly removed the mask. My face was burning up. I'm not usually a blusher but by now I was as red as a beetroot. The kids sat in stunned silence. Even Helga was lost for words.

'I can't believe I just did that.'

Nor could they. I think some of them were as embarrassed as I was. Then the room erupted. The kids rolled around in hysterics while I looked for somewhere to hide.

That was the last time I ever attempted to perform *commedia*. It was, however, the beginning of a wonderful relationship with that class. We had a lot of fun together and I think they might have learnt a bit as well. They had seen me in a vulnerable, compromising position and we shared a laugh at my expense. As crazy as that moment was, it cemented our mutual trust. If I could make a complete fool of myself, why couldn't they?

I virtually ran to their classes from then on, even when I wasn't running late.

In service

My reintroduction to the high-school world continued on playground duty. PGD. At a school like Newtown it seemed a total waste of time. There were never any fights. The worst thing that could happen was someone might fall off their pointe and injure their toe. But duty of care is duty of care! With nothing else to do I sat on a bench and enjoyed the sunshine.

I couldn't help but overhear the very animated conversations that were springing up all around me. This was something else about the kids at Newtown: they didn't see the need to censor their behaviour when a teacher was in the vicinity. They were too self-obsessed. This isn't necessarily a criticism – it's a universal teenage condition, and you'd expect performers to have a bigger dose of it than most. Of course, some people never grow out of being obsessed with themselves. A lot of them become actors.

These kids seemed incredibly confident about many things, particularly their physicality. They seemed far more relaxed about their bodies and in touch with who they were than any kids I'd ever taught.

Sitting there in the sun I may as well have been invisible. There was a group of little Year 7 dancers sitting and stretching nearby. They were, like most kids, all talking at once. They were stereotypically blond and there wasn't a hair out of place among the lot of them. They were innocence personified. Butter wouldn't melt in their mouths – until they opened them.

'Fuck off.'

'She fucking said what?'

'What a fucking bitch.'

'I love your fucking hair.'

'Yeah, it's fucking awesome.'

'Fuck that was a hard class.'

'Fuck yeah.'

'Fuck.'

I couldn't believe my ears. This wasn't Tenterfield. These kids hadn't ridden in from the mountains. They were little princesses, yet when they spoke they were like Year 7 kids the world over. And these were the dancers – you should have heard the musos! In fact, I was amazed to find that many of the things I had parodied in *Us or Them* all those years ago were still evident even in a school like Newtown. The outside world may have turned upside-down but at school a good deal of time was still spent in staff meetings discussing smoking in the toilets, chewing gum and school uniforms. It occurred to me the kids at Newtown might look and sound a bit different but they were essentially still kids.

The six-week block flew by and I had a ball. Newtown was an extraordinary place to work. For someone like me who loved the world of theatre and performance it was like I'd died and gone to heaven. I was combining my two great loves, teaching and drama. So when Mel offered me more work the following year, I jumped at it. I replaced Groucho who was taking the year off to look after his new baby. There was obviously something in the water in that staff room because when Groucho returned Vanessa went off to have a baby. I spent several years subbing people who were reproducing. It allowed me to pursue my other interests as well as feed my own kids more than just sausages.

When St George's Hall was ready and the dance staff had moved in, the three disciplines of dance, drama and music all had their own buildings. Drama now had three specially designated studios all to itself. It was incredible.

My Year 11 class graduated to Year 12 and it was to be the first experience I'd have of teaching at that level. There were four Year 12 drama classes at Newtown, which meant more than 80 kids doing the HSC exams. It was big but it was to get bigger. Before long there would be five Year 12 drama classes: 100 kids.

Teaching HSC drama was demanding, exhilarating and stressful all at the same time. The stakes were high, as Helga kept reminding me, but I loved teaching it. I had 25 kids in my class; each did an individual project and they all did the group one. There were two topic areas, one of which had to be Australian. They had to study two works in each area, which meant that for the written exam they had to have four works under their belt. Drama was no soft option.

One of the plays we studied was Bob Maza's *The Keepers*, which was a nice bit of circularity; he'd mentored me at Eora and now I was teaching his play to white kids in Newtown. I was blown away by how open-hearted the kids were. It wasn't just because they were doing performing arts; as far as reconciliation with Indigenous Australia was concerned, this generation of kids was way ahead of their parents, not to mention the politicians. I told them about my experiences at Eora, how I'd listened to first-hand experiences from the Stolen Generations. I could never tell that story without tears, but it didn't stop me telling it. Years later I took my Year 12 to Sydney University to hear Prime Minister Kevin Rudd make the official apology to the Stolen Generations. It was without doubt one of the highlights of my teaching career to share that cathartic moment in Australian history with a new generation of kids.

I'd got an idea about the pressures of HSC performance from marking, but it was only an inkling. Each kid needed shepherding through their 'IPs', as the individual performances became known. This meant helping them select the piece and advising them, but not directing them. It was a fine line to tread. Teenagers can be pretty demanding at the best of times; put them in a really stressful situation with high stakes and equally high expectations and you get a pretty explosive cocktail.

All 25 of my students wanted a piece of me at once. Some took my advice, some didn't. If kids had their heart set on a comedic piece when they didn't have a single funny bone in their body, there wasn't much I could do about it. If they wanted to wear a silly beard and deliver their lines in a fake English accent, I had to give them all the encouragement I could muster. When 'Grace Kelly' chose to play an Indigenous character I quietly suggested that it seemed an odd choice for a non-Indigenous woman. She was rare; she took my advice and started again. And she got top marks.

The group performance was challenging from the moment the groups were chosen to the day they were performed. Everyone wanted to work with the 'stars' and Newtown was full of them. Often the happiest groups were the ones in which the kids weren't friends and had never worked together. The stuff they came up with was remarkable. Using contemporary theatre techniques and often incorporating song and dance, they cast a critical eye over the world they lived in, taking on everything from consumerism to the environment to body image to race relations and more.

When it came to the big day I was like every other drama teacher in the country. I was more nervous for my kids than I often was about my own work. Maybe the stakes were higher? What made it particularly draining was that I had 25 opening nights to sit through, without counting the five or six groups. And I had to exude calm; I could hardly go to the bar and down a couple of quick scotches before the show.

In those days the groups performed first. During each performance I was like a punter at the track 'riding' a horse home. After the first group finished we'd celebrate and then another one would be up and I'd ride them home. When it was time for the IPs I'd do the same again for all 25: I'd laugh and cry and burst with pride, then damp it all down for the next one. It was an incredible ride and it made every second worthwhile. Sometimes I wondered if it meant more to me than to the kids. That's teaching.

During that first year of taking a Year 12 class I also marked HSC performances. In fact, I'd been promoted to a senior examiner. My job as an 'SE' was to call in on the marking teams and make sure everything was under control. I drove from one end of the state to the other, seeing all sorts of schools and assisting markers wherever I could. It was magic.

The first week of marking was in the city, which was just as well because my Year 12 were scheduled to perform their IPs and GPs that week too. However I was scheduled to be at a prominent Catholic girls school on the day of my kids' performances. How could I be in two places at once? I managed to make up some excuse at marking, race across town and hide up the back while my kids did their stuff. Then I raced back to where I was meant to be. I couldn't miss my kids' performances – it'd be like missing the birth of your children.

There were a few teething problems in those early years of HSC drama, before all the teachers had a handle on the examination requirements. At the same prominent Catholic school a group of girls was doing a clever piece about body image. It was a very intelligent work of Brechtian-inspired drama. However at one point they started taking their clothes off. I was busily writing down marks and ticking off skills when I looked up and realised what was happening. They were making a statement about societal pressure on young women. I got the point and assumed they would stop at the bras; after all, it was a Catholic school. I kept writing feverishly. However it soon became obvious they weren't going to stop. They were going the full monty. I wasn't sure where to look – the girls were standing only two metres away. The two women sitting next to me marking were similarly perplexed. The piece ended and we breathed a collective sigh of relief. It was a very brave, confronting piece of drama but it did lead to a ban being placed on nudity. In those early years there were some tricky moments with naked flames and starting pistols too!

It was a great time to be involved in HSC drama. Led by Mel and Vanessa, we were trailblazers for the subject. Because its candidature was still relatively small, it was also quite informal and relaxed. Both kids and teachers loved it. But drama was the fastest growing subject on the curriculum and its spectacular growth coincided with increased levels of formality. I was soon asked to report on my fellow markers' conduct and dress; they were now required to wear suits and ties and 'formal attire'. We were reminded that we represented the department. What was this, 1950?

It seemed an odd contradiction to me to mark performances dressed up like a character from *Homicide*. In my final year of marking I was sent to Byron Bay, which was great except that everyone thought I was from the drug squad. I saw the writing on the wall. It was time to give up marking.

Third period

As I settled into teaching Groucho's classes I became more and more aware of the life and culture of the school. For instance, I learnt that two-thirds of the kids were chosen by audition. They came from all over Sydney and all over the state, and many spent hours travelling to and from school.

The school's location exposed them to a world that was far removed from the one most of them grew up in. It was situated a couple of blocks down from Newtown Station, which was a hive of all sorts of nefarious activity, especially on pension day. Every morning a chorus of blond, bouncing, bright-eyed, pony-tailed dancers would hop off the train, giggle their way up the steps and out onto King Street past junkies, dealers, drunks and assorted ne'er-do-wells. Kids coming from all points would arrive at school having negotiated the full gamut of inner-city life. They didn't seem to bat an eyelid. I often wondered if those parents who worried about their angels mixing with kids from the local area were aware of what they were witnessing at Newtown Station every day.

There were kids from the bush who boarded with relatives or friends. Others found their own accommodation. Two of the girls in my Year 12 class, who arrived at the school in Year 11, were living with billets. I thought that was pretty extraordinary for kids who were only 16 and 17 years old. A lot of students lived in ways their teachers could barely imagine.

The one thing that united them all was a fierce determination to go to Newtown and to perform. I'm not sure how many still wanted to perform by the time they left school. Maybe in Year 7 it had been their dream; it was certainly the dream of a lot of their parents. The truth was, after six years of performing the majority would never grace a stage again. But that didn't matter – Newtown wasn't a 'little NIDA', despite what some people imagined. It was a school that taught an incredibly high level of performance skills. It produced many fine performers and many more socially aware, confident kids who had adored their school days.

Aside from the audition kids, one-third of the school population was made up of local kids drawn from the local area. In that way Newtown was quite unique – it was a selective high school that also served the local community. Selective schools were once drawn from geographical areas, such as Sydney East or Sydney North, but at some point the boundaries were removed and anyone from anywhere could get into a particular selective school as long as they got the marks required. It opened a can of worms: parents began crawling over each other to ensure that their kid got into the highest-ranked school, in the mistaken belief that it would set them up for life, and schools lost their connection with the local community.

I thought the mix was Newtown's greatest strength. It meant most of the kids who auditioned didn't get too far up themselves, while the local kids got to mix with talented and highly motivated students from elsewhere. It was win–win for both groups. I believed that kids from the local area could become as good at drama as any of the audition kids. The issue of 'audition' versus 'local' was one where Joan and I parted company. She wanted the school to be 100 per cent audition-based, as did some of the other performing arts teachers. Joan didn't agree with my position but she respected my right to hold it.

It was an issue that split the staff. Although Newtown had been established as a performing arts high school, it still functioned as a normal school offering all the usual subjects. There was inevitable tension between performing arts and other departments. This was highlighted when kids were rehearsing or performing and missed classes in other subject areas. It came to a head when big performances such as a state festival clashed with assessment tasks. It was a very tricky path to negotiate. Parents rightly expected their kids to get the best mathematics teaching possible but they often had to balance this with their child's desire to perform in a big concert. It drove the teachers who taught subjects outside performing arts mad. They were expected to get good results out of their kids even though they would miss so much class time performing.

Interestingly Newtown's overall HSC results stacked up pretty well. Not that looking at a school's ranking could tell you much you didn't already know. Highly motivated, intelligent, middle-class kids were likely to do well. That said, the myth that kids need to spend their teenage years with their heads stuck in a textbook was well and truly exploded by the results. It seemed that kids who are happy and motivated are likely to do well wherever they go to school. The busier they are, the better they'll do. They're kids after all – they have heaps of energy. Being in a drama company was no more of a handicap than being in a hockey team.

Everyone can gain from drama and music in the same way that everyone can gain from sport or physical exercise. Asking kids to limit their horizons when they are still teenagers is crazy. Just look at the problems professional athletes who were targeted and hothoused from childhood encounter in later life. Our world is a complex one and our job as teachers is to prepare kids for a rich and diverse world, not a homogenised and narrow one. The broader the school experience, the richer the society.

I expended a lot of energy convincing the local kids that they were as good as the audition kids. I told them that if they kept on auditioning they would eventually end up in a company. I was confident about this. I managed to get an acting career through sheer persistence. I even got to star in a movie. If I could do it, they could too.

Being in a company was a big deal at Newtown. It was the coolest thing you could do – way cooler than smoking in the toilets. The companies were chosen by audition. The kids had to prepare a two-minute monologue to perform for the teachers. As there were more kids than places, inevitably some had to miss out. I taught a girl called Skye in Year 7 who absolutely loved drama. Skye tried and tried but unfortunately she kept missing out. I suggested she join the costume company but she had her heart set on performing. I tried to convince my colleagues to give her a go.

'She can't act.'

I couldn't believe my ears.

'Can't act? She's a kid.'

'She's hopeless.'

'But—'

'I couldn't understand a word she was saying.'

'She was nervous.'

'Next.'

Skye didn't make the cut. The result? She lost interest and went off the rails. It was inevitable. I didn't have her in my class in Year 8 so I only saw her in the playground. I tried to joke with her, to keep the lines of communication open, but it didn't work. In the end I think she resented me. In some way I'd let her down because she'd trusted me and I hadn't been able to deliver. My best intentions had led to expectations that weren't met. Unfortunately the disbanding of ensembles meant that kids like Skye never got to perform on stage in front of an audience. I though it was a pity.

I never bought the argument that performing classwork for the public created more work, quite the contrary. And it gave more kids a go.

In Year 8 all the kids were mixed in and I often wasn't sure whether a kid was 'local' or 'audition'. I could pick the musos, but only because they all looked like they had fallen out of Frank Zappa's tour bus. The rest fell into the melting pot and most of them did drama.

I had one rule. If someone was having a go, everyone in the class had to show them respect. They had to support them. No talking or mucking around. Of course, one kid tried it on. A girl was doing a particularly intense piece of character work in a Year 9 class, and this boy started making inappropriate sounds. The rest of the class started giggling.

'Please.'

'What?'

'Give her a go.'

'I wasn't doing anything.'

'Just be quiet.'

She continued. She was struggling but that wasn't the point. The boy tried it on again. His mates were egging him on.

'Do that again and you're out.'

'What?'

'You know perfectly well.'

'I didn't do nothing.'

'Your choice. Another sound and you leave.'

'You can't send me out.'

'Watch me.'

'You've got to give me warnings.'

'I just did.'

'Three.'

Bush lawyers. This guy knew the 'correct procedures' better

than I did.

'See that door?'

He looked at me quizzically.

'You talk while someone else is performing and you can grab your bag, head out the door and catch the next train home.'

'You can't ...'

I'd learnt something at Tenterfield. I called his bluff.

'I can. And I have.'

He didn't know if I was serious or not.

'Come on, we've got work to do. What's it going to be? You going to shut up or piss off.'

I swore. His language. I didn't do it deliberately, it just came out. There was a moment, then he grumbled and sat down. He never said another word.

There were many times in teaching that I might have said or even done something that could be regarded as inappropriate. I certainly swore from time to time. I got so totally absorbed in the subject matter that I might have even dropped the F-bomb. The kids hardly noticed. A lot of the plays we studied included characters who swore – it was no big deal. Most of us, kids and teachers, were too into what we were doing to be worried about trivialities such as swearing.

Besides, kids had changed. Language had changed. Behaviour had changed. And kids weren't stupid. They knew their teachers swore, their parents swore, the characters in their favourite shows swore. And we won't talk about the music they listened to. Why didn't the system acknowledge this? The hypocrisy was breathtaking and self-defeating. 'Fuck' was no longer a taboo word – it was everywhere. And it was hard to avoid swear words when the Board of Studies prescribed texts that were full of them. So when a teacher reprimanded a kid for saying 'fuck', the kid often didn't know what the fuck it was for. It wasn't the word that mattered so much as the intention. The little dancers weren't using the F-bomb to shock or be rude or challenge authority; they were speaking their language. Now I think about it I never swore with Year 7 or 8. Maybe I was more relaxed around my senior classes?

The junior kids at Newtown were unlike any other kids I'd come across before. They were as motivated as kids at a birthday party, one that had costumes and props and heaps of fun things to do. Only this one went on for a whole year. When I asked Year 8 to 'walk through mud' in a movement class, they did. When I asked them to 'walk on the moon', they did. If I'd asked them to climb out the window and lie down in the middle of King Street they probably would have done that too.

However, 'motivated' doesn't begin to describe the new Year 11 class I was allocated. They were theatre tragics. A number of them have gone on to have outstanding careers in the entertainment business, including running major theatre companies. Many of them were part of Vanessa's A-team. She couldn't teach all of Year 11 so the unlucky ones got me, with Vanessa overseeing what was happening. From time to time she would burst into my room and read the riot act to the class. We'd all take notice. A problem arose once companies were allocated and one of Vanessa's star performers ended up with me. She was distraught. I was thrilled; she was really good.

'Hi, Evita. You're in my company.'

She grunted.

'I'm so pleased.'

'Are you?'

'Yes. I thought we'd have a shot at *Top Girls*.'

'Yeah?'

'It's a great play. You'll love it.'

It is and she did, but she took a bit of convincing. She later went on to become a director.

It's a tough gig following a popular, charismatic teacher, especially one the kids are attached to. It takes a while to win their trust. You can only do it by being yourself. There is no point trying to be someone else. That's the trouble with a lot of teachers; they try to be someone else and the kids see right through them.

One of the boys in that class was a freak. He was a scrawny little thing with big glasses and a brain the size of Uluru. We got on really well, even if I struggled to keep up with him. The only thing I knew more about than he did was cricket. And only just. When he asked for my feedback on the lighting design he did for a show he set in St Andrew's Cathedral, I just nodded.

'It's great. Very ... evocative.'

'Of what?'

'Of what you're ... you know ... trying to achieve.'

He pushed his glasses back on his nose and went to Hendo for some decent feedback. When he topped the state everyone congratulated me. Me! As if I'd had anything to do with it. Mickey Mouse could have taught that boy and he would have topped the state.

Teachers are, by their very nature, adaptable. A high school teacher will often teach pre-pubescent kids who are 11 and 12 as well as young adults who are 17 and 18. In terms of adapting, I had to really step up to the plate with the senior classes at Newtown. For one thing they thought they knew as much, if not more, about performing than I did. It didn't matter how many plays I'd written or films I'd been in, they'd been in six companies at Newtown. The number of times I was told:

'That won't work.'

'I'm not doing that.'

'The audience won't get it.'

I'd patiently reply, 'I know, I'm stupid, but do you mind if we try?'

They'd roll their eyes.

'Do we have to?'

'Humour me.'

They'd walk out at the end of the class or rehearsal muttering:

'How come we got him?'

'I know.'

They'd throw me a glance. They wished they had Vanessa. They got the rough end of the pineapple with me. I had a long way to go to win their confidence.

One day in company I brought in Kasey Chambers' song 'Not Pretty Enough'. The piece we were devising was about self-esteem and it seemed perfect. One girl fixed me with a look that said, 'You've got to be kidding.' I asked them to improvise some movement to the song. They parodied it. It was beneath them. That is, all except one girl who ended up choreographing a dance sequence to the song. She performed it on the night and it brought the house down.

I was old enough and silly enough not to be too bothered by their contempt for my ideas. It was part of the gig. These kids were convinced they were heading for the bright lights. No doubt kids at sports high schools assume they'll make it to the Olympics too.

It was interesting and very challenging teaching these 'A-type' personalities. My prior experience of teaching had been with a whole range of mixed-ability kids. I prided myself on helping them reach their potential, whatever it was. I knew I was good at getting students to believe in themselves. I got students of all ages to achieve results they thought were beyond them. I loved getting someone across the line who thought they'd never get there.

This was different. These were kids who, on the surface, were pretty sure of themselves. They weren't short of an opinion and they were quick to dismiss my suggestions or to challenge my assertions. I loved this. It kept me on the ball. A major challenge was finding the right thing to say. I couldn't say, 'That was total shit,' regardless of whether I thought so or not. Instead I'd go for, 'Needs some work. Maybe learning your lines will help?' And nor could I say, 'That's the best thing I've ever seen,' because, of course, it wasn't.

A large percentage of the work students did in drama was unsupervised, particularly in the senior years. Given that the HSC involved the students creating a group performance on their own, which required them to meet up and work together outside school hours, it was important they learnt this discipline at an early age. In fact, most of what all years did in drama involved working in groups. After they'd been taught the theory, students would get together and put it into practice. It was a wonderful platform for life. It taught self-discipline and commitment. No matter how hard they'd been partying or how shitty they felt, kids had to turn up at rehearsals for the sake of the group. And they'd spend hours rehearsing, after which they'd show me their work and I'd give them feedback. It was always detailed and a lot of it was politely ignored.

As I was still working as an actor, there were times when I needed to audition. This meant finding time for it in a very busy schedule, and taking a day off wasn't an option. I'd try to arrange the audition for when I had a senior class. I'd make sure they were all busily working in their groups. Then—

MR MANNING, *firmly*
Carry on!
Runs out the door, down the stairs, into the Kombi, across town to the audition, back in the car, back up the stairs and back into the classroom. Continues lesson.
Okay. Let's see what you've got?

After this little performance I'd be gasping for breath, heart pumping, pretending to be cool as a cucumber.

'Can we have more time?'

'What?'

'We need to go over it once more.'

'You're kidding.'

'Please?'

Why had I run all those red lights? Rhetorical question, of course. I'd shrug.

'Oh, all right.'

Funnily enough the kids were convinced I had disappeared into one of King Street's many coffee shops. They never knew I was halfway across the city trying to remember lines. Doing what they were doing and, not surprisingly, doing it badly.

I hasten to add that I never did this with my junior classes – that would have been abrogating my duty of care – and I soon stopped doing these mad dashes across town altogether. I don't know what I was thinking. It was hardly the best way to prepare for an audition; nor was it the most responsible teaching practice. If an audition didn't fall outside class time, I didn't go for it. On the other side of the ledger, keeping one foot in the acting door meant that I never lost touch with just how hard it can be. How exposing, even humiliating. And how soul destroying it is to be constantly rejected. This is why I objected so strenuously when someone put a kid's performance down or, worse, dismissed it out of hand.

While my theoretical knowledge of drama was a bit light on, my experience as an actor stood me in good stead when it came to practice. It was second nature for me to analyse work and iden- tify problems. I loved watching performances and trying to work out how to improve them. I never tired of talking about acting, although some of my kids may have grown tired of listening. As for teaching playwriting, I learnt a lot more than I taught. In those classes, *I* was the kid at the birthday party.

I tried to share some of my knowledge of the professional world with my senior kids. I didn't talk about myself much or carry on about my work. They would have torn it to shreds. It was bad enough when YouTube was invented and someone posted a particularly embarrassing scene for all to see, or when someone was sick at home and saw a rerun of my early performances on daytime telly. It was unavoidable that the kids would notice when I was in an ad or an episode of *All Saints*. When *Looking for Alibrandi* came out I got lots of 'Like a cup of tea?' Good-natured piss taking.

I never talked about me 'doing' the actual work but I did try to warn them about the pitfalls of a professional life. I spoke about the arbitrary nature of the game. I urged them to 'follow the dream' but to also be prepared for plenty of knock-backs. I talked about how they needed resilience, determination and luck. I told them about co-ops and producing their own work, and that this was the path they would have to take if they wanted to work in the industry. They looked at me like I was mad. As if they would have to do co-ops!

It was very naïve of me. Most of them didn't want to know about the real world. They didn't want some curmudgeon bursting their balloon. I learnt that pretty quickly and I was almost never asked for advice.

I wrote and produced a play called *Milo* and it was being performed at the Sydney Theatre Company's Wharf Theatre. I'd done much of the production work for it in the staff room, when no one was around, of course. I should have acknowledged the department as co-producers! I didn't say much about it to the kids. I was too busy keeping them on track with whatever we happened to be doing at the time. And I'd learnt that even motivated kids will happily seek out diversions. It was hard for them not to notice it though, as there were posters all over Newtown announcing the upcoming season. One of the drama staff thoughtfully organised an excursion to the matinee. It wasn't compulsory but a lot of the seniors booked tickets to go along.

'We're coming to your play.'

It was more of a challenge than a statement.

Milo had garnered good reviews. It was doing well and I was pretty happy about it. I was pretty bullish, in fact – until the matinee loomed on the horizon. I was happy for the support but I was scared shitless at the thought of how the kids would receive it. What if they thought it was crap? I was sure some of Vanessa's A-team would. What about the other drama teachers? They'd told me how much they hated naturalism. When I'd mentioned that Currency Press was publishing a catalogue of Australian plays, one of them had proclaimed:

'There's never been a decent Australian play written.'

Mmm. And I was an Australian playwright. I must have been off my rocker. When it came to bagging a play these people made the Sydney critics look like philanthropists.

D-day arrived and I fronted up to the Wharf to see half the senior school lined up at the box office. I nearly died. I tried, unsuccessfully, to appear nonchalant. What I had done hit me like a ton of bricks. I'd put my credibility on the line. I was beginning to understand that being a theoretical expert about theatre was one thing, but putting that theory into practice in public was quite another.

I rode every laugh, every cough, every murmur, every yawn. I panicked when they didn't laugh. I was paranoid when they did. When they shifted in their seats I thought they were going to walk out. I couldn't bring myself to look at Vanessa. I knew she'd hate it. It was an absolute nightmare.

Then it ended and they all clapped. One of the actors called me onto the stage for a Q and A. The kids gave me a standing ovation. I nearly burst into tears.

Back at school we carried on as though it had never happened. Years later, when *Milo* got a bad review, someone thoughtfully photocopied it and dropped it on my desk.

The relationship between drama teachers and the profession was a weird one. More than once I heard a teacher boast that their school production of a play was better than the professional one.

'You've got to see it. It's much better than Belvoir St's version.'

'The acting is so professional.'

'Yeah. Our kids are so great.'

I don't know why school drama wanted or needed to compare itself to professional theatre. Did the community at a sports high school believe their netball team was better than the Australian team? I doubt it. The school community was rightly proud of the fantastic achievements of their kids but they didn't need to elevate them to levels they couldn't hope to reach.

Once when a kid missed a rehearsal his teacher told me:

'He'll never work again.'

Work? He was a kid doing a school play.

The problem was that many people in the school community only ever saw school performances. I threw myself into my productions as much as anyone but I never for a moment believed they were anything more than really fantastic school productions. To suggest the kids were at the same standard as professionals, people who did it for a living, was clearly absurd. All it did was give them unreal expectations. They thought they *were* working. They thought their work *was* better than what they saw at the Sydney Theatre Company. They thought they were a shoo-in for admission to NIDA.

A lot of kids felt terribly let down when they discovered, to their surprise, that they weren't the stars they believed they were or dreamt of becoming. When they missed out on drama schools I can only imagine how they suffered when they closed the door of their bedrooms and contemplated the terrible reality that they might not be actors after all. It must have been awful. It's one thing to make kids feel good about themselves. It's quite another to give them false expectations.

This is not to denigrate the kids' efforts or the incredible gravitas they brought to their performances. But it was up to the adults to provide a bit of perspective. How could the kids be expected to have any perspective at their age? They hadn't lived enough yet.

The music department had a lot of input from outsiders: professional musicians. I saw quite a few of my heroes rushing across the playground to give tutorials in one musical field or another. I even ran into the composer who had done the impossible and taught me singing for a play I did with the Sydney Theatre Company. If she could teach me I knew she'd have a field day with the kids at Newtown. The music department seemed to embrace their profession. Their tutorial program was extensive; it was good for the kids and good for the musos. For a kid to be tutored by a legendary trumpet player like James Morrison or a rock star like Tim Freedman was pretty special. The musos loved it because performers love passing on their craft and sharing their knowledge. It's part of being a performer.

There were teachers, on the other hand, who would jealously guard their turf. Some drama teachers weren't even interested in seeing theatre outside the school, which was very odd. How could you keep up with contemporary theatre practice if you didn't see contemporary theatre? We had 'outsiders' from the profession come in and direct companies but I never felt they were entirely embraced. And when a professional company came to perform at the school, it was almost like they were trespassing. I never knew what that was about.

My place on the staff became an issue when one of the drama teachers resigned and a full-time position was up for grabs. Joan suggested I apply for it. I wasn't keen. I'd found the perfect balance between teaching and my 'other' career, or so I thought. In reality I was still a casual and I couldn't rely on a succession of pregnancies to provide me with employment forever. Sooner or later I'd be out of a job. Here was the classic conundrum created by a system that couldn't find room for professionals. How could I commit to a full-time teaching position when I'd worked so hard to establish myself as an actor and a writer? I knew I was just starting to hit my straps. Teaching had given me some of the training I'd missed out on, and I still had a lot more to learn. I loved the kids, I loved the school and I loved teaching, but the bottom line was I couldn't give up acting and writing. I told Joan.

'You don't have to worry about that,' she said.

'What do you mean?'

She winked. She was inscrutable.

'I'll look after you.'

She handed me an application form. I knew Joan was as good as her word so I took it home and packed my bags for the holidays. I filled it in and sent it off and never gave it another thought.

When I got back to school Joan accosted me in the playground.

'You didn't fill it in properly.'

'What?'

'You forgot to sign it!'

She nearly killed me. As it happened another drama teacher had burnt out and another position became available; Joan made sure I signed it and I got the gig. I was back full-time teaching. I was happy as a pig in shit, living the best of both worlds.

I soon had a chance to put Joan's promise to the test. I was cast in an ABC series called *The Farm*. It was a great role with one of my favourite directors, Kate Woods. Even though Joan had promised it would be okay I was nervous that I wouldn't be able to get leave. It was more than a couple of days; it was a few weeks away on location. By this time Mel had moved on and Vanessa was head of drama. We'd developed a really good professional relationship. We'd sparred, we'd shared classes (and tears), we'd even done a show together. As soon as I was cast in *The Farm* I rang her. I was really worried. I had my heart set on this role. This was the first real test of my ability to juggle two professions.

'That's fantastic, Ned.' She was genuinely excited for me.

'Will it be okay? I'll leave work for all my classes. Year 12 are—'

'Don't worry about that. We'll cover you.'

And she did.

My next hurdle was Joan. What if she reneged on our deal? What if she couldn't fiddle the books? I knocked on her door. There was something about knocking on a principal's door that still freaked me out.

'Isn't it wonderful? Vanessa told me. Now …' She started flicking through a huge folder. 'Yes. Professional development. How long will you be away?'

'Three weeks.' I winced as I said it.

'Good-oh. Now about this playwriting course …'

That was it. I was over the moon.

I don't know how Joan arranged it but I got paid for both jobs. Her rationale was that I would bring professional experience back to the school and into my classes. She was right. I got to sharpen my skills and test myself in the real world. It was awesome! *The Farm* remains one of my most cherished roles. It was a subject dear to my heart and I loved my character.

There was another reason why it was so special. When I fronted up for the first read-through I was pumped. I'd prepared well and was ready to rock. We sat around the table and before we started we said our names by way of introduction. It was just like at school.

'Ned Manning.'

Then I turned to the young girl on my right whom I hadn't met.

'Yael Stone.'

Yael Stone!! She was in my Year 9 class. I nearly fell off the chair.

'Yael?'

'Mr Manning?'

We both blushed. Being the pros we pretended to be, we carried on with the introductions as though this was the most natural thing in the world. But I found it difficult to concentrate. How was this going to play out? We were going to be on location together, hanging out in a caravan, eating out, socialising. She was playing my 'son's' girlfriend. We'd be doing scenes together. It was pretty crazy.

Yael gave up calling me Mr Manning for the shoot and, not surprisingly, was a total pro the whole time. She was also very good. We had a ball.

While the shoot had been seamless, it was a different matter when we got back to school. Yael was in my class for drama and extension drama. Both of us tried to carry on as though nothing had happened. It was way easier for me – she had to slot back into being a teenager after being treated like an adult. Some of the other kids were already jealous of her. We bumped into each other in the playground and talked about how we were both back in our old roles again: I was the teacher, she was the student. If she hadn't been mature beyond her years it could have been tricky. Without favouring her I looked out for her and made sure she got to do some directing, which gave her something different to focus on. Yael was arguably one of the most talented kids to go through the school and definitely one of the most humble.

When *The Farm* came out the deputy came up to me – yes, in the playground – and with tears in his eyes told me how proud he was of my performance. I'm not sure anyone had ever said anything like that to me before. I was knocked out. It was a beautiful thing to do and it meant the world to me.

After doing *The Farm* I bounded back into the classroom. I was refuelled and raring to go. I attacked my classes with renewed vigour. My teaching was all the better for having spread my professional wings. There is no doubt that my classes benefitted from it.

Years later, long after Joan had retired, I ran into the question of 'professional development' again. Things had changed and I wasn't nearly as confident of getting leave. The new boss was a stickler for the rules, which is probably one of the reasons he got the job. Chris had been an economics teacher and found himself in the curious position of being appointed principal in a performing arts high school. Undeterred, he threw himself into the job.

7-ON, a company of writers I was part of, had a workshop at the Sydney Theatre Company. There was a chance it might lead to a production. I decided to bite the bullet and go to Chris about it. If I'd been slightly apprehensive about Joan I was shitting bricks about seeing Chris. And I was pissed off that I was shitting bricks. What the fuck was a guy my age doing getting nervous about knocking on a principal's door? Hadn't I grown out of it yet? This was ridiculous. Chris wasn't intimidating but he wasn't one to beat around the bush either. I knew I'd better get this right.

My opening gamut was to argue that if teachers who were also representative athletes could get leave to pursue their professional careers, then why couldn't professional artists? I also pointed out the ways it could benefit the school.

Chris patiently listened to my argument. To my eternal relief he saw my point. He didn't offer me 'professional development' but he trawled through the *Education Act* to find the relevant legislation. He was slightly different to Joan in his approach. He turned his computer around and showed me the Act. It was written just after Cook had landed in 1770. The section we were looking at hadn't been amended since performing arts high schools were invented; nor had it been amended since the annual City versus Country

Rugby League game was a jewel in the representative crown and teachers who were picked were given leave to play. I think the last of those games was in the 1970s, maybe even before I went to Tenterfield.

Chris agreed that his staff would benefit from working in their chosen profession at the highest level and that these benefits would be passed on to the kids. He suggested I approach the Teachers' Federation for their support. He was an example of a leader with vision, perhaps even a bureaucrat with vision. Put a reasonable argument to him and he would act on it.

I approached the federation with confidence; after all, they represented teachers. Surely they would support the idea. I wasn't arguing for special privileges; all I wanted was for us to get leave *without* pay and to not lose our entitlements, such as those related to tenure. The Fed Reps appeared to see the logic in this. They said they would get back to me. For some reason they were suspicious of performing arts high schools. I think it had something to do with Marxist philosophy and selective schools.

Word came through that they would approach the department with my suggested change to the Act. I waited. And waited. And waited. When I eventually got hold of them they told me the department wasn't interested. Typical bosses. I tried to find out exactly who they had talked to so I could put the argument myself. This drew a blank. Uh oh. Déjà vu, Tenterfield 1973.

I didn't want to die of old age before anything happened so I decided to cut to the chase and go to the Minister for Education. She happened to be my local member so I rang up and got an appointment the next day. Within a week I had departmental approval for the proposal. If I got work I could take leave without pay and without penalties. It would take a while to change the Act but in the interim I could have my 'professional development'. And I had Chris to thank for it.

I've also got Chris to thank for my brief excursion into the world of teaching languages. I didn't speak any foreign languages. At times I struggled with English. Chris had come up with a scheme whereby kids coming into the school at Year 7 would have half the number of new teachers to get to know. In primary school they had the one teacher for a whole year so the transition into high school, with a different teacher for each subject, was a tough one. It was a great idea. It also meant that teachers would have to double up and teach two subjects to Year 7. One would be their subject of choice, which in my case was drama, plus one other subject such as history or English or PE. Sorry, PDHPE.

I volunteered for this scheme. To stave off complacency – or was it boredom? – I volunteered to have a shot at most things. I coached the cricket team, I directed the annual tribute to Year 12, I coached a girls touch-footy team, I was the race-caller at the swimming and athletics carnivals. I'd do anything except be the staff representative at P&C – parents and citizens – meetings. That would have been death by a thousand cuts.

The first year this scheme for Year 7 was trialled, I put my hand up for P**** or whatever it was called. Sport. It went okay. It was more PD than PE; more sex education than running around the oval. I didn't realise it would be so much 'chalk and talk'. I wasn't up for discussing 'personal development' with 12- and 13-year-olds.

The next year I was allocated two Year 7 drama classes: 7A, which was the dreadful name they gave the local kids, and 7Dr, the kids who'd got in for drama. To keep myself on my toes I decided to not only volunteer for Chris's scheme again but to volunteer to be year adviser as well.

I had the bright idea that I could teach French as my second subject. It was only one double a week: one lesson, 80 minutes. I could handle that, no sweat. Then I made an interesting discovery. In Year 7 kids at Newtown got a double dose of languages, in this case French. In Year 8 they got none. If they were interested in languages they could pick them up again in Year 9. It was one of Joan's more eccentric decisions. So by the time I'd signed up I realised that I had 7A for twice as much French as drama. And the classes were split into three. One double, 80 minutes, and two singles, 40 minutes each. On top of that they were all in different buildings; they weren't even in the languages block. By some twist of timetabling logic they were in an art room, a geography room and a history room respectively. This meant I couldn't even leave my technical equipment – vital for my survival – in the classroom but instead had to lug it all over the school. I'd finish a drama class, grab my goods and chattels and hurtle across the playground to find the building in which I was meant to conduct my French lesson. It was pure Clouseau, and like Clouseau I wasn't laughing as I stumbled around, although I think everyone else was.

I omitted to mention that I had failed HSC French outright. My appalling skills had improved since then, but not enough to cover a load like the one I was burdened with.

'Bonjour la classe.'

'Bonjour monsieur.'

'Ça va?'

'Ça va bien.'

When I ran into Chris on the way back from one of these circuses, he smiled.

'Careful what you wish for.'

I didn't know what this meant but he was lucky I was loaded up with books, cassette recorders, DVDs and the rest of the paraphernalia I needed to survive. Otherwise I might have decked him. Despite my best efforts it remains unlikely that anyone from 7A will be majoring in French at the Sorbonne.

I took my job as year adviser seriously. We had meetings,

discussed kids' problems and did our best to make their transition into high school as smooth as possible.

At the end of the year we had an 'Elders' Day' for 7A. It was one of the best days I had at the school. It was a chance for the kids to show a parent or grandparent or family friend what they were doing at school – and a chance for the local kids to show that they could kick a few goals too. They performed some drama, read examples of their work in various subjects, displayed their artwork. They put on morning tea and we even planted some trees, although I can't recall us doing any French.

The true worth of Newtown is illustrated in the story of a boy who had been to quite a few schools, many of them private, before he found his home there. At most schools he had been a fish out of water; he found it difficult to relate to other kids, he'd been bullied because he was different and he couldn't get on with his teachers. He was an unhappy kid and his parents had run out of options. He pleaded with them to let him audition for Newtown at the end of Year 10. The one thing he was confident about was his love of the arts. He also thought that he stood out. That was until he hit Newtown.

He later told us about how he arrived at school, after having spent hours getting his hair right, and sashayed across the play-ground waiting to be noticed. All anyone cared about was what company he was going to audition for and what he had to offer. For the first time in his life he was free from having to define himself by what he looked like or where he came from or his sexuality. No one cared. All the things that had caused him grief at other schools were irrelevant at Newtown. He was free to be himself and his life was transformed. He threw himself into the school and was as happy as Larry. When he told us that story it was through tears of gratitude.

Newtown was the safest environment you could imagine for

kids who might have been different in one way or another. Difference was not only tolerated, it was celebrated. The school had a reputation as a 'gay school', which might have been stretching the truth. It also had a reputation as a 'druggy school', which was so far from the truth it was laughable. There were drugs at Newtown just like there were drugs in all schools, but there was a lot less evidence of drug-taking than I'd come across elsewhere. It's hard enough to remember your lines if you're off your face, let alone balance on your toes.

Before I knew it, I'd spent what seemed like half a lifetime at Newtown. It's funny how time flies when you're having fun. It was a long way from the portable at Tenterfield to Drama One on King Street.

Groucho had become a head teacher by now and he offhandedly asked me if I'd be interested in going to China. The school's dancers had been touring America for years and Chris thought it was time music and drama showed their wares off overseas. I say that Groucho was offhand because I don't think he thought I'd be interested. Vera, our resident physical theatre expert, had pulled out at the last moment. It was looking bad because no one wanted to go. I was the last man standing. Groucho was actually heading out the door to beg an English teacher take the drama kids when he asked me.

'Can I get back to you?'

'I need to know tomorrow. The boss wants to get it sorted.'

I went home and told my wife that I had the chance to go China.

'Fantastic. When are you going?'

'I dunno. I wanted to ask …'

'Are you mad?'

My wife was an adventurer from birth. I went into school the next day and told Groucho of my decision. He nearly fainted.

Epilogue:
End of term

We're standing in a car park waiting for the bus. It's raining. By now a few of us have cheap plastic raincoats. We've been shopping in the Yu Yuan Market, which is a huge market in Shanghai geared for tourists. While the kids haggle over five-cent raincoats I slip away for a bit of a walk around the less-touristy laneways. I love China – I love the extremes of sight and smell. When I return we roll out the two most asked questions of the tour:

'Where's the bus?'

'Where's Wally?'

Chris is standing there as raindrops fall gently on his shoulders. He's arrived because ... I'm not sure why he's here, but he is the principal and he is fitting in well with Team Ned. The day he arrived he asked me:

'Where's Team Chris?'

I smiled.

The last few days have been frantic. After Expo we've performed each day on spaces ranging from a postage stamp to a grand theatre. One member of my team was too sick to perform at the Shanghai Oriental Art Centre but the show went on all the same. It had been billed as the big-ticket item of the tour, a joint performance, although we never had any contact with the Pudong students we were meant to be 'joining' with. They were bussed in and out and we were given a corridor for a dressing room. In fact the only time we really had anything to do with our hosts was when we played basketball with some kids after a visit to one of our many 'sister' schools. It's a pity, but we go with the flow.

Our performance at the Shanghai Oriental Art Centre kept us indoors for nine hours until the pre-show 'tech' was done. When we finally broke out for some much needed fresh air, we crossed the park and joined a group of elderly men and women who were doing some kind of therapeutic dancing, a weird fusion of Tai Chi and the Macarena, to the strains of someone like Mariah Carey. The kids gave me their cameras and bags so they could join in the dance. I must have looked like a parody of an American tourist with all that paraphernalia hanging off me. They were having so much fun I decided to join in, bags and all. That was how Chris and Bobby found us when they arrived; Bobby is the new deputy and the sole member of Team Chris. I'm not sure what they made of our communal dancing in the park but it gave them a taste of things to come.

The kids are lapping up the cultural experience. They're also getting used to performing wherever, whenever. Blackouts occur indiscriminately in the middle of our performances but the kids take them in their stride and wait for the lights to come up again before continuing the show. And after every show there are ban-quets. We have banquets coming out of our ears. Even if it's nearly midnight, we'll dutifully file in to wherever the banquet is held and take our places, our heads nodding off into the congee. The truth is we're having a great time. We've become a family. It's pretty special.

We've survived four days in Shanghai without losing anyone. We've walked along Nanjing Road and been up the Jin Mao Tower. Not only have we not lost anyone, incredibly we haven't got lost either. But Wally, our tour guide, has. And so has the bus driver, which is why we are standing in the rain being hassled by street-sellers who've swarmed to us like bees to a honey pot. Finally the bus arrives. We climb aboard and we're off to Yangzhou.

The bus trip is remarkable: the scenery is breathtaking and so is the driving. Our driver thinks he's on the speedway. If the kids' parents were worried before we left they'd be having conniptions now. Not content with impersonating a Formula-One driver, he also talks loudly – very loudly – on his mobile. The kids are exhausted but it's hard to get forty winks with someone shouting into his phone. It's even harder when he lights up a gasper and fills the bus with smoke.

The kids smile. They're getting the hang of this tour thing. In fact I get the distinct impression they're pretty happy to be outside their comfort zones. Every minute offers something new – no wonder the tour is called 'Expanding Horizons'.

When we reach our destination we alight and make our way to our dormitories. We're staying in a school, which is more like it. The Chinese kids, who are incredibly welcoming, have given up their rooms for us. We've hooked up with the other schools from the Sydney region who make up the tour party: another 100 kids and their teachers. Two department heavies have also joined us, although there's nothing heavy about them. They're both great, if constantly frazzled. They're the ones who have to deal with the nitty-gritty of touring China with 200 kids and 20-odd teachers.

After dinner we settle into our wooden bunks for a well-earned rest. It takes me a while to get to sleep but a few discreet shots of duty-free scotch do the trick. I'm sleeping soundly when the door is flung open and Bobby rushes in.

'Someone's been electrocuted!'

'What the …'

'No time to talk. I'm sleeping in here!'

He chucks his bag on the spare bunk and disappears. I'm not sure if I'm dreaming. He reappears and grabs his bag.

'It's all right. There's a spare ...'

He doesn't finish the sentence and if he does I don't hear it, or understand it. I roll over and go back to sleep.

We awake to the news that a girl from one of the other schools unplugged the air conditioning to plug in her hair straightener, and her hair got straightened more than she expected. It just seems like a dumb thing to do, but it's taken as a cue for some hysterical over-reacting. The tour leader summons us to a meeting and informs us that we're moving out.

'But we've just moved in.'

There's a bit of argy-bargy and Dylan and I are pretty unhappy. Our kids are loving being in an authentic Chinese school environment. Why should they be punished? And it's hardly our hosts' fault if this girl was so silly. 'Owning your own behaviour' springs to mind.

There are all sorts of wild accusations, including the Chinese kids looking through the windows when the girls were changing. We were in a separate building – you'd need binoculars to look in here – and there were bathrooms they could change in, but none of this seemed to matter.

It transpires that some of the other schools aren't enjoying the experience anywhere near as much as we are. Oh well, tough. What did they expect? But our protestations fall on deaf ears. One in, all in. Or in this case, one out all out.

What really pisses us off is that the Chinese kids have given up their rooms for us, and our kids are desperate for some real interaction. Why should we move back to a hotel just because a couple of teachers can't handle being in China? I begin to wonder what they're doing here in the first place.

Notwithstanding, we have a great day at another 'sister' school.

We participate in classes, a couple of our kids get made up in traditional Chinese opera costumes, we play some traditional instruments. Someone gets very confused and thinks I'm a music teacher. They insist I play for them and they won't take no for an answer. With cameras whirring I sit down and give them a rendition of *The First Noël*. My signature tune, the only one I can play. They smile. God knows what they are making of this. Our kids are rolling around the floor laughing their heads off. I've damaged our school's reputation irreparably – but don't tell anyone ...

We then discover that we are not only watching a concert but we're supposed to be performing in it. Okay. As we walk towards the hall I'm frantically trying to work out what we're going to do. Due to some quirk of bureaucratic logic we are without four students. Four of our company had to go to another school because ... I don't know why! All I know is that we're on. I gather the remnants of Team Ned around me.

'Guys. We've got to perform.'

'We haven't got our costumes.'

'That's okay. You've done it before ...'

'I haven't got my clapping sticks.'

'We haven't got our bamboo sticks.'

'Come on. Remember Expo? You slayed 'em in the aisles.'

They weren't laughing.

'But we're missing half the company.'

'That's an exaggeration. Only a fifth.'

'But—'

I put my foot down.

'Do you want me to jump in?'

Ha ha! Hilarious. A few look at me like I might be serious.

They perform of course. It's a bit strange as they waltz with ghosts and try to work out who is missing from which bits, but it doesn't matter. The Chinese love it and I am one very proud 'dad'.

From that day forward we never go anywhere without our costumes and our sticks.

We watch the Chinese kids perform their bit of Chinese opera. They are decked out in full regalia: make-up, stunning costumes, the works. Their athleticism is incredible. We are all drawn to one boy whose focus and intensity are hypnotic. He inhabits the characters he is playing. I gather the kids around.

'Did you see that?'

'It was amazing.'

'What about that boy?'

'Wasn't he awesome?'

'His focus. I couldn't stop looking at him.'

This is the type of lesson a million words can't teach. My guys get it. They've seen what they need to aspire to if they are to live the dream. It's the very best kind of lesson, when the teacher doesn't have to say a word.

When I talk to the Chinese teachers they tell me the director/choreographer of the piece is a professional, brought in to tutor the kids in this centuries-old art form. One of the Chinese teachers makes a really interesting observation.

'Your kids could learn from our precision and we could learn from your ability to enjoy yourselves on stage.'

He's right. Our kids are looser and less paranoid about making mistakes. The Chinese kids' discipline and attention to detail is faultless. It's interesting that wherever we play we bring the audience to their feet at the hip-hop moment – it's slightly cheeky, a hell of a lot of fun, and it's kids being kids.

After the obligatory banquet we head off to visit the Old City of Yangzhou before returning to our host school for dinner. We walk in and see tables laden with Kentucky Fried Chicken. We're thinking 'What the fuck ...' as we survey the mounds of junk. The principal of one of the schools we're travelling with pats herself on the back.

'I ordered it,' she proudly explains. 'After the disaster last night I put my foot down. My girls are over the food. I told them we ...'

I walk away. I can't tell her she's an insensitive fool. I can't kick up a fuss because our hosts have gone to so much trouble and are beaming at us, whatever they might really be thinking. I notice my kids are two steps ahead of me.

'Don't say anything. Just eat it.'

'But it's so rude,' says Lily.

'I know.'

It's the low-point of the trip and it gets lower when we find out that everyone else has been treated to banquets of local food. We're a funny people, us Australians. We can be so generous and so mean-spirited all at the same time.

The low point continues to plummet when we return to the school to collect our bags. It's late and we're exhausted but, because of one girl's idiocy and her teacher's myopia, we can't hop into our bunks. Oh no. It's onto the buses and back into town to a 'nice hotel'. I could scream. Everyone gives me a wide berth as I toss the bags and instruments back on the bus.

Then a golden moment.

Our kids have decorated their rooms. They have left thank you cards and presents for the Chinese kids who gave up their rooms. Totally unsolicited. All off their own bats.

Awesome.

The rest of the trip is a string of unforgettable moments. Tours of historic sites and travel on planes, trains and ... buses. School visits. Banquets, banquets, banquets. Performances in theatres grand and humble. Magical experiences like the Shaolin Temple, the Shaolin Gung Fu Institute and the Dengfeng Markets. Our kids cover themselves in glory and open their eyes to an unimagined world.

We've all bonded strongly and turn towards home with mixed emotions: happy to see friends and family, but aware that we've been part of something very special. It will stay with us for the rest of our lives.

My teaching career, in this incarnation, is drawing to a close. My final act is a production of Nick Enright's classic *Blackrock* in St George's Hall. It's a great way to bring down the curtain on my years at Newtown. It's also full of the kind of emotional connectivity that I love. Nick was a very dear friend. He introduced me to my wife at the gates of the school when he'd come to do some research with some of my kids. We did *Blackrock* as part of Year 10 classwork, culminating in a performance of the whole play in which each class performed allocated scenes. Nick came to see a couple of these mini-productions.

I've always wanted to do a full-on production with kids. *Black-rock* is a play about a teenage party that goes horribly wrong. I'd only ever seen it done by adults pretending to be teenagers – good productions but lacking the kind of truth only teens can bring to their stories. A lot of my 'China' kids are in the show so we've already got a wonderful shorthand. A couple of music kids I'd got to know in China are doing the music. A student from NIDA, Emma Kingsbury, is co-ordinating the design with some Year 11 kids. A couple of Year 10 girls are overseeing everything backstage and some amazingly reliable Year 8 kids are working on the set. This is what it's all about – kids doing a play about kids with kids running the show.

When it's all over, of course, I'm going to end up in tears. I'll be incapable of putting words to what I feel. I'll possibly have a drink or two when I get home and I'm gonna be really grateful for all the years I've been teaching.